ACTA UNIVERSITATIS UPSALIENSIS
Studia Doctrinae Christianae Upsaliensia
27

David Jenkins

The Scope and Limits of John Macquarrie's Existential Theology

UPPSALA 1987

Distributed by:
Almqvist & Wiksell International
Stockholm — Sweden

Doctoral Dissertation at Uppsala University 1987

Abstract

Jenkins, D., 1987: The Scope and Limits of John Macquarrie's Existential Theology. Acta Univ. Ups. *Studia Doctrinae Christianae Upsaliensia* 27. 154 pp. Uppsala. ISBN 91-554-2005-2.

This dissertation examines in depth the problems involved in applying John Macquarrie's existential methodology to issues in theology. It focuses on the epistemological issues, opening the discussion with an analysis of Macquarrie's concept of truth. The author argues that an existential methodology ends up making it impossible for a theologian to refer meaningfully to the empirical, factual aspect of knowledge. Existential phenomenology reduces knowledge to knowledge about the universal structures of Being, which do not themselves give information about the factual conditions of the world or about history. The author explores this thesis in respect to Macquarrie's understanding of science and history, illustrating the difficulties of his thought with essays on demythologization, interpretation, speculation, and Christology. The author finds elements of a solution to Macquarrie's difficulties, however, in various threads of thought that run through his works. He isolates Macquarrie's notion of a "domain" of thought, capitalizes on his untended commitment to the value of empirical experience, and develops his notion of a "language-game" into a fuller and more functional concept of domains of knowledge. The author preserves the validity of existential-phenomenological thought by making it one aspect of a domain, which develops in "tensional" dialogue with the other aspect, the concrete, empirical "pole" of a domain. He distinguishes a number of different domains, showing the basic mechanisms by which a domain is established. Finally, he points to the rich and complex matrix of religious epistemology by showing how domains interplay between and among themselves to achieve progress in their respective domains. Thus, the religious domain interplays with those of science and history (as well as many others) to make knowledge-claims which legitimately include empirical as well as phenomenological-existential aspects of knowing.

David Jenkins, Department of Theology, Uppsala University, Box 1604, S-751 46 Uppsala, Sweden

© David Jenkins 1987

ISBN 91-554-2005-2
ISSN 0585-508X

Phototypesetting: Textgruppen i Uppsala AB
Printed in Sweden 1987
Graphic Systems AB, Angered

Table of Contents

Introduction 7
Truth 14
Summary and Critical Conclusion 20
Degrees of Truth 26
Science 33
The Problem of History 47
The Problem of Historical Facts 49
The Existential-Historical and the Objective-Historical 54
Interpretation 59
The Resurrection 64
John Macquarrie's Phenomenological Ontology 70
Language 88
Conclusion 107
Final Words: The Interplay of Domains 126
Appendix A: Bultmann 135
Appendix B: Demythologization 138
Appendix C: Macquarrie's Stand Against Speculative Thought .. 143
Appendix D: Christology 146
Bibliography 153

Introduction

One of the most influential Christians in the world of philosophy and theology today is Oxford's Lady Margaret Professor of Divinity, John Macquarrie. As the co-translator of Martin Heidegger's *Being and Time*, Father Macquarrie early made his mark as an influential proponent of Christian existentialism. He has been one of the few existential thinkers who has not been reluctant to identify himself as both Christian and existentialist. He has written most of his works with the aim of incorporating much of what he deems of Christian value in Heidegger's philosophical anthropology into Christian theology. He has also found useful the ideas of other existentialists, such as Karl Jaspers, as well as elements of the Thomistic tradition; and his theology represents an attempt to formulate a Christian existentialism which touches nearly every major point of the faith.

I first encountered the works of Macquarrie at the age of 18 when I entered college in the United States. During the summer prior to entering school, I read the master work of this early writings, *Principles of Christian Theology*. I chose to read this book in order to balance my reading of Augustus Strong's very think book laying the foundations of Baptist theology, his conservative, fundamentalist *Systematic Theology,* with which I had been struggling during the preceding year. I wanted to know how a "liberal" theologian would treat the major doctrines of the Christian faith. The result was that I gave up the legalism and Biblicism of my Baptist faith and became a proponent of what I took to be the correctly "philosophical" faith. I entered college with a resolve to study philosophy, one of the few resolves which I have managed to carry through to a successful end in my life.

During my college and graduate school experience, philosophy absorbed my life. I read widely in the history of philosophy and devoted myself to a close study of its many themes, topics, and problems. I cannot say that I lost my Christian faith during this time so much as that I *lost track* of it as my mind was overwhelmed with topics upon which to reflect. The issues to which I was most attracted as problems to reflect on, however, were no doubt generated from my previously more conscious and explicit Christian commitment. I was interested in the problem of God, in the problems of philosophical anthropology, and in the nature of belief and faith as epistemological problems. I chose to write my master's thesis on the problem of intersubjectivity, defending the position of Gabriel Marcel over that of

Jean-Paul Sartre. And, in the course of writing it, I rekindled, through my acquaintance with Marcel's writings, an interest in existentialism as a philosophical tool for dealing with problems in explicating Christian faith and doctrine.

During this time, I rediscovered the works of Macquarrie. I have to say that at this time in my life my reading of several of Macquarrie's works led me to feel that I could not go on any longer as a philosopher without taking responsibility as a Christian to speak as a *Christian* philosopher. Perhaps I felt this way because I saw Macquarrie doing it so well and resolving so many of my perplexities about Christian faith. I felt that Christian faith, properly explicated, could answer many otherwise empty philosophical questions. Macquarrie made it possible for me to identify myself as a Christian with a mission to "think out" the faith.

I ended my movement toward a doctorate in philosophy with a master's degree and spent the next three years earning a Master of Divinity at Duke University in North Carolina. I entered seminary with the aim of studying Christian faith and doctrine so that I could return to doctoral studies in religion and eventually emerge into the academic community as a well informed and penetrating defender of Christian philosophy. And, when my mind was again overwhelmed with scores of conflicting theories and ideas, a return to a reading of Macquarrie's works was again clarifying and helpful in integrating Christian thought.

But other experiences in seminary began to exert influences on me which weakened Macquarrie's hold on me. The powerful socratic teaching of William Poteat, a master of Wittgenstein's philosophy, challenged me to cease doing "ontology" and get to the "bedrock", where all explanations come to an end. One of the prime American proponents of liberation theology, Frederick Herzog, awakened my consciousness of new developments of Christian moral theology, developments which demanded action rather than explanation and theory. I came out of seminary without a clear direction and with some confusion concerning how to formulate a Christian philosophy.

I returned to study for a doctorate in philosophy at Loyola University of Chicago, where I wrote a dissertation under the influence of Michael Polanyi (philosopher of science, author of *Personal Knowledge*) on social ethics. My study of Polanyi confirmed my direction away from existential thought, as I formulated an epistemology that was somewhat inimical to the pure phenomenology that grounds existential thought. My application of this epistemology of "tacit knowledge" to ethics ended in the formulation of a complex of ideas which were critical of the existential approach to philosophical problems.

My prime philosophical problem now became how to re-integrate the insights of existentialism with this new development in my philosophical thought and how to relate this integration to a philosophical explication of the Christian faith. A couple of years in the mission field and in traveling the world gave me time to reflect on this problem, even if it gave me little time to write on it.

I have entered into this study of Macquarrie's thought, under the auspices of the doctoral program at Uppsala University in Sweden, with the honest hope of finding a way of re-integrating Macquarrie's form of Christian existentialism into my philosophical thought. And I believe that I have succeeded in doing so, at least to an adequate degree. But the success of this dissertation does not really turn on whether I have achieved such a personal ambition. It turns instead on how well I have been able to show that existential thought (and the phenomenology that grounds it) has definite limits in explicating Christian faith and that, if it is to have a place at all in theology, it must be corrected by an approach that preserves the empirical, factual element of theological thought that forms part of the meaning of every Christian's Easter affirmation, He is risen! Thus, the formulation at which I arrived in the course of my study of Macquarrie ended up being more critical than I at first intended; but I think that it is only in the light of the critique I present of Macquarrie that we can see the validity not only of what he tries to do as a Christian philospher but of how one might utilize his positive contribution in the development of a different approach.

I argue in this dissertation that Macquarrie, even though he is well aware of the problem and intends to avoid it, falls into the Bultmannian error of reducing the factual claims of Christian thought to existential interpretations. I procede with the assumption, which Macquarrie himself makes, that Christians mean what they say in the ordinary sense of the word when they say that Jesus was raised from the dead, or that he did this or that in his life (with important theological consequences), or that God is active and present in their lives. We must, of course, agree with both Macquarrie and Bultmann that such assertions of faith must find their explication and deepening of meaning in a phenomenologically grounded existential interpretation. We naturally want to know what the affirmations of Christian faith *mean* for human existence. And we can go a long way with both Macquarrie and Bultmann as they unfold the intricacies of an existential interpretation of many of the knotty problems and concepts of Christian theology. But Macquarrie recognized that there is a limit to demythologizing and argued in his book on Bultmann that Bultmann had fallen unwarily into the trap of existential reductionism. Macquarrie himself argued that we must take history seriously as Christians. But—in each instance in which he ought to make some sort of pronouncement concerning how we can make historical claims as theologians, he wavers: he either says that he doesn't wish to formulate a philosophy of history or else he ends up remaining satisfied with interpretation, with a statement about what a claim *means* for human existence. Thus, I argue that he falls unwarily into the same trap he insists Bultmann has fallen into. And he compounds this error by choosing to label any attempt to transcend the trap of this reduction of a claim to its meaning for human existence as "unwarranted speculation", which always ought to be avoided in theology.

I argue, on the contrary, that, if we are to take Macquarrie's affirmation of the importance of factual, historical claims in theology seriously, we must find a way to speak of them which does not end up reducing them to "meaning". Thus, what I have tried to do with Macquarrie's thought is to push forward this claim which seems very important for explicating what Christians really mean as they explicate their faith and show how it can be validated in the context of the rest of Macquarrie's thought. It turns out that Macquarrie's affirmation of history is something of an empty claim that has no further function in his thought than to pay heed to the need to note it. It runs counter to the rest of his thought, even if he means it when he makes it. So my task in this dissertation is to show how Macquarrie's thought can be modified and corrected in order to pay proper attention to this claim as well as to the program of existential interpretation to which Macquarrie is committed. The success or failure of this work should be judged on the basis of how well I have managed to accomplish this task, and not on how well I have introduced a new methodology to theology. In this work, I am only showing how Macquarrie can be modified and corrected by a theory which I only outline here, which I call "mutually confirming and correcting cross-referencing" of "domains" of thought. I believe that my concept of cross-referencing of domains of thought preserves Macquarrie's assertion that the empirical, factual side of our knowledge claims are essential aspects of them while freeing us to engage in phenomenological investigations and existential interpretations which deepen the significance of these facts for us. A consequent notion which derives from this methodology is the value of what Macquarrie denigrates as "speculation". Because of the continuous interplay and interpenetration of the various domains of thought with each other, no reasonable manner of investigating a problem in theology or any other domain of thought need reach a dead-end. I.e., even when evidences are lacking in one domain to make a final, resolving statement on some matter, so that the matter seems permanently closed to further fruitful investigation, disclosures from the vantage point of *other* domains of knowledge can change this situation. We are never, except in the cases of genuine mystery and paradox, able to settle a matter by saying that nothing is left but "idle speculation". To do so may be correct as a temporary matter of fact; but its sin is that it locks the thinker into an improper attitude toward any object of inquiry: it invokes the attitude that we can know that we *cannot know* certain things which are in fact not inherently unknowable but which merely lack adequate evidence for a legitimate claim at this time. I think Macquarrie falls prey to this attitude when he ends up agreeing with Bultmann's existential reductionism. I argue, on the contrary, that we must, as far as is reasonable and possible, keep all inquiries in theology open, even when no immediate answer seems available. For we must enter into the interplay of thought within and between domains with a spirit of adventure and discovery, a spirit which might at any time turn up something relevant to a solution of a problem in *any* domain. Thus, history, science, ethics, anthropology, etc., all interplay to produce hitherto unexpected and unintended insights which become relevant to all sorts of problems, including those which vex us in the domain of religion.

I will briefly inform the reader of my strategy in developing the thesis of this dissertation. I begin with a discussion of Macquarrie's notion of truth, showing how deeply indebted he is to Heidegger's notion of truth as *aletheia* and to the Thomistic tradition. I distinguish three levels of *aletheia* in his works: (1) everyday, pre-reflective engagement in normal human activities, (2) reflective modes, consisting in phenomenological-existential knowledge and the empirical knowledge of the sciences, (3) the level of "thinking Being", in which we grasp Being through symbols which transcend the connections of thought common on the second level. The chapters on science and phenomenological ontology unfold the meat of Macquarrie's epistemology; the third level of *aletheia* is described in the context of a "transcendence" of the second level toward symbols in language which "catch us up" into Being and allow us to "think" it.

The consequences of Macquarrie's emphasis on the second level of *aletheia* are immediately applied to some important theological problems: the problems of the nature of historical facts in theology and of their relationship to theological hermeneutic. I note here that Macquarrie falls into existential reductionism. In order to illustrate the degree of trouble which this way of thinking implies, I have appended some brief essays on various topics, including a statement of Macquarrie's relationship to Bultmann and his program of demythologization, a description of how Christological doctrines are affected by Macquarrie's ambivalent position, and a note on Macquarrie's position on speculation in theology. Although these essays are included as appendices, they are very important for understanding my critique of Macquarrie. The copious footnotes which follow each chapter also contain very important material for understanding the strategy and aim of this dissertation, and they should be carefully studied.

The third level of thought is taken up in a chapter on Macquarrie's theory of language, which represents a third philosophical strand of Macquarrie's philosophical-theological synthesis: his commitment to take into account the theories of language, in particular language about Being and God, developed by the British analytic tradition. He adopts a number of linguistic theories from this tradition, and I have tried to show how they influence his way of expressing ultimate notions of Being and of God. The Wittgenteinian concept of "language-games" and "family resemblances" are in particular integrated into his philosophical theology.

My response to the problems which I discern in Macquarrie's approach to philosophical theology is to introduce a theory which I believe makes it possible to preserve much of what Macquarrie has achieved in integrating these various strands of philosophical influence together into a synthetic whole without, in any obvious way at least, falling into the difficulties in which he finds himself. The notion of mutually confirming and correcting cross-referencing both *within* and *between* (or among) domains of knowledge leaves intact the individual criteria for knowledge claims in each domain, while it "opens" each domain to *relevant* judgments in other domains. These judgments are relevant in the sense that maintaining them implies that one must maintain or must modify or delete judgments in other domains, even if quite different criteria are functioning in each domain. Undergirding what I designate as a free, interplaying cross-referencing activity among or between domains is a secondary interplay between the empirical, factual, concrete aspect of any knowledge claim and its explication and contextualization in terms of a phenomenology which is valid within a particular domain. The interplay *within* a domain, which I call "inner, tensional cross-referencing", takes place between these two aspects of any knowledge claim and establishes the organic unity of a domain. Free, interplaying cross-referencing *among* domains themselves (of which there are an unspecified number) makes any effort to understand any one domain an adventure in which the various judgements we make along the way are never final and never close the matter in any final way. This does not mean, contrary to the spirit of critical thought, that we end up knowing nothing. We are, in fact, *committed* to the notions that we hold, and they act as heuristic guides to new discoveries; we know *something* of reality, a something which can be most adequately expressed in terms of the total picture we have available at this time. We ought not to fall into the sceptical trap of saying that we do not know *any* truth since nothing is apodictically certain or evidentially verified in a final way. We have a partial grasp of the truth from a number of differing perspectives, and we are in the process of emerging into a deeper and more profound grasp of the truth within each domain of knowledge and, if philosophy does its job well, of reality as a whole. Our attitude should be one of a willingness to keep any matter not obviously discredited in its worth of pursuit open to investigation. This implies that important ideas, ideas upon which our values and goals in life turn, have a legitimate claim on our willingness to remain open to consider them. Instead of believing that they are discredited as soon as they seem incompatible with one or two domains of thought, we should remain open to evidences which might turn up in other domains of thought, evidences which might confirm their validity, at least in a limited way. This is not to say that we never ought to reject ideas; I am saying only that rejections ought never to be viewed as closed matters and that, in the case of ideas which are so important that our goals and values turn on them, we ought actually to engage in an active search for evidence which confirms or finally corrects or discredits the ideas. But this active search in other domains is nothing other than what Macquarrie often disparages as speculation. I believe he does so, however, only because his philosophy lacks this element of legitimate adventure which I add to it.

Truth

One cannot approach John Macquarrie's philosophical thought without noting, at least briefly, the influence of Martin Heidegger on him. Macquarrie makes no secret of his being heavily indebted to the thought of Heidegger. Indeed, an analysis of his epistemology will reveal that Macquarrie's thought is deeply grounded in that of Heidegger. I will not enter here upon a discussion of all the Heideggerian influences on Macquarrie's thought, nor will I attempt to show in detail how Macquarrie's thought differs from that of Heidegger. Although such a study might be historically interesting, it is both unnecessary and irrelevant in this work. Macquarrie himself clearly footnotes his open appropriations of Heidegger's thought and clearly distinguishes his position from Heidegger when he strikes off in his own direction.

One can, however, describe the general tenor of Macquarrie's philosophy as Heideggerian, a characterization which includes elements of both the early and the later Heidegger. In respect to the recent debate concerning whether the early and the later Heidegger are in contradiction, Macquarrie, who appreciates both periods of Heidegger's thought, sides neither with those who claim discontinuity nor with those who claim continuity between the two periods. Clearly linking Heideggerian thought with a basis for Christian thought, Macquarrie claims that Heidegger's movement through existential self-understanding (the early period) to primordial thinking (the later period) provides a contemporary way of understanding and expounding the notions of mysticism, contemplation, and revelation.[1] The early and later Heidegger stand to each other in a dialectical relationship, each complementing and correcting the other, but neither able to be fused with the other in a new synthesis.[2] Macquarrie clearly affirms that the whole of Heidegger's thought (and theistic forms of existentialism in general) can be relied upon as avenues to a contemporary reasonable ground of Christian faith and thought. Nonetheless, we will see that Macquarrie is no slave to continental thought and that he uniquely appropriates and interprets other philosophical traditions such as Scottish idealism, British analytic thought, and Thomism.

Macquarrie's conception of truth, however, follows closely that of Heidegger: He says,

> "The most fundamental meaning of 'truth' is uncovering, or bringing to light. Truth is *aletheia* (my transliteration), unconcealment, so that we speak truly if what we say lights up what is talked about and shows it, as far as possible, without con-

cealment or distortion. But to light up anything in this way is to let our minds 'appropriate' it, in the sense of making it our own and incorporating it into our understanding".[3]

Macquarrie is not proposing a theory of truth that is intended to compete with other classical theories such as the correspondence theory, the coherence theory, the pragmatic theory of truth, etc. He is saying that, *whatever else* we might say about truth or whatever method we might follow in establishing its criteria, *any* theory of truth presupposes an original uncovering of the object under investigation. We might ask whether our concept of the object agrees with reality, or whether it is consistent with our view of reality as a whole, or whether it makes any difference in our daily lives; but none of these criteria for speaking the truth about the object (whether it is a physical object, a theory, a value, etc., makes no difference) becomes possible unless the object first becomes *present*, is uncovered or disclosed as the object that it is. The disclosure of the object is the ground for the possibility of any truth statements concerning it and any criteria that may be employed to establish their truth. We must, eg., see *man* as the being he is, i.e., let him be *disclosed* to the inquiring person, before we can explain *why* he is what he is. We can argue for the validity of our interpretation and explanation only on the basis of truth-criteria that presuppose this primordial disclosure.

The deepest truth of an assertion, then, is not its agreement between thought and reality but the disclosure of the entity as it is (*aletheia*). Concealments and distortions have been removed,[4] and that which is can be seen as it is. Understood as "unconcealment", truth is an event of appropriation, a "living-in-terms-of" an understanding which throws light on a situation.[5] That truth is an event of appropriation means that it has a personal dimension, that it is a truth *for someone*. This, in turn, means that it is something we *rely* on, find *trustworthy*. The unconcealment of an object of thought is inseparable from the total life-context in which it takes place, in which we invest our lives; it involves our total way of being, the disclosures that constitute our fundamental and primordial grasp of reality. It is, in fact, quite proper to say that truth is basically *a way of being*. For its appropriation requires our taking up a new relation with whatever we have counted as most real, a relation which demands a restructuring of our being so that new truth can emerge and have its place. *The* truth is never present all at once; but the temporal process of its appropriation procedes to a more complex grasp of a reality which is always present in some respect, even if only through a deception which invites us to "find out" the truth.[6]

"Primordial" truth is a process of personal appropriation of insights which light up our total situation as truth-seekers and human beings. It is always culturally and historically conditioned, since there can be no final formulation of "the" truth. But this admission does not constitute a lapse into a rudderless relativism: Being *is* present in every situation, and its truth is always more or less adequately emergent via the vehicles of language which enclose the situation. The yet-unread truth of Being invites us to advance beyond the deceptions of our present situation, to move toward an understanding that will never be complete and yet whose end-point is always revealed in terms of this invitation.

Macquarrie's concept of truth involves a recognition that truth cannot be identified with what we ordinarily count as "objective fact". It must include the personal and communal dimensions of an inwardness that is aware of its freedom and responsibility for the "truth-character" of the world that appears in the context of our openness to it.[7]

This distinction between "objective facts", such as those proposed in the sciences, and the "truth of Being" is grounded in Macquarrie's view that human existence is a more fruitful revealer of being than the objects and the causal relations which obtain between them in the scientific world. In other words, Macquarrie is committed to a form of existentialism.[8] He says,

> Existentialism . . . denies the claim of that school of thought that the only knowledge is that which can be scientifically verified, and affirms, on the contrary, that scientific knowledge is only one kind of knowledge, not privileged but specialized, and subordinate to the fundamental knowledge, which is knowledge of existence.[9]

It would seem from this statement that existentialism in valued as a good medium for expressing insights into human reality which make no sense in the world of scientific realities, a world that is inadequate for giving such an understanding. Grounding truth in an understanding of human existence yields ever fuller interpretations of Being, interpretations upon which we can rely through a continuing process of confirmation. In this way, existential philosophy provides an ever-widening structure of intelligibility and meaning.[10] The sciences are merely a "specialization" of this sort of knowing, which is intended to provide the stable theoretical structures in which all domains of human knowledge, including the sciences, participate.

The epistemological beginning point in any inquiry, then, ought to be an analysis of our own existence, which always lies open to us.[11] This includes laying out for view the structure of the being of man and showing how this differs from the being of objects of nature; and this project leads to the develop of a terminology dealing with Being.[12] This analysis of human existence cannot and does not remain merely a disclosure about the existence that pertains to being human. Human beings live with some understanding of Being; their existential structure always involves a disclosure of Being which has a meaning that transcends the human structures themselves. Knowledge of existential structures always involves, to some extent, knowledge of the fundamental ontological structures of Being. Existentialism leads naturally to ontology. Indeed, Macquarrie indentifies ontology with an analysis of the ontological presuppositions of an inquiry into existential structures.[13]

The project of clarifying existential structures is a commitment to discover the meaning of Being. As such, it naturally discloses the manner of our "givenness" in the world in terms of our commitments. The search for truth is a way of giving ourselves in the world, of existing, of commiting ourselves. As such, it remains open to the modifications which the in-breaking of truth brings to old forms of understanding, even though these "old" forms are themselves the vehicles of language which bear, beyond their own ken, the new. Thus, understanding is not just an "intellectual" act: it is a fundamental way of being in which the person takes up the project of understanding.[14]

Macquarrie, agreeing with Heidegger,[15] says that understanding is an existential, a category which expresses a possible way of being. He defines an existential in the following way:

> An existential possibility is one which is revealed by existential analysis and which belongs to *all* human existence in virtue of the way this existence is constituted. An *existentiell* possibility is one which is open to me *in a particular situation* so that I can decide for it. All *existentiell* possibilities must lie within the horizon of existential possibility; but there may be existential possibilities which are not *existentiell* possibilities for a given individual at a given time.[16]

An existential, then, is a category used to describe man as he is in his essential structure as a human being. Existentiell possibilities, on the other hand, describe the elements of a person's particular situation. Existential structures, however, are not to be understood as pre-given, immutable, "natural" structures. They, too, are possible ways of being, free and open structures whose content is determined by the fundamental choices of the person. As an existential, understanding, e.g., is a praxis which invests things with a meaning in order to find itself in a world of sense. It is the content of these commitments or investments of meaning which forms the ground of the categories in terms of which we understand the world. These categories are the *theoria* of our lives and are the source of the distinction between what we count as "objective truth" (e.g., the sciences) and "subjective truth" (e.g. feelings, wishes, etc.). What we count as truth, whether "objective" or "subjective", is the product of specialized projects of understanding, all of which are grounded in and are not supposed to be inimical to the understanding we gain of our existential structures.[17]

Existentialism, then, as a "tenor" of philosophy, acknowledges that the process of coming to know is itself part of the ontological dynamic of the person. Focusing on how we come to be aware of our world and forming theories about it lead directly to an understanding of the Being that grounds both this process of understanding and that which is understood in it: Being.[18]

This interplay between our specialized categories of understanding, such as those developed in the sciences, and the existentials disclosed as the meaning of Being points to a more profound unity of truth than is suggested by the normal hodgepodge of seemingly unconnected truths which confront us in everyday life. Indeed, Macquarrie circumscribes the relativities of what seem to be different sorts of truth with a concept of unity. Truth, indeed, is multiform: there are different kinds of truth for different dimensions of experience, all of which need exploration and clarification concerning the criteria of truth that are proper for each dimension. But Macquarrie insists these differences need to be viewed as the various forms of a higher unity of truth. He does not view this unity as a homogeneous, rigid structure. But he believes that there is a "family resemblance" to other kinds of truth.[19] I.e., each domain of truth (history, politics, religion, etc.) may have its own content and its own criteria for determining what is true in its sphere, but it also has elements in common with one or more other domains, each of which is connected with the other either directly or obliquely by similar relations. These interconnections create a loose kind of unity which falls short of being as "essence" of truth which might define truth "essentially" in every domain of human understanding. This loose unity is never complete and always invites us to discover a closer knit through a dialectical process which never yields an absolute, final truth.[20] In conclusion,

> The truth is not found in a final consensus in which all can rest—and especially not in a consensus so broad or so vague that it is devoid of interest and almost of meaning. Truth is not something at which one arrives, but more of an ongoing process, involving the interplay of different views which sometimes correct each other, but which defy all attempts to subsume them into a single truth.[21]

In summary, this section has dealt with Macquarrie's fundamental notion of truth. Grounded deeply in the thought of Martin Heidegger, Macquarrie's concept of truth is intimately bound up with the themes of existentialism. Truth is *aletheia*, or "unconcealment". As such, it is an event that takes place in the human person, an event in which the person trusts, commits himself, and lives in terms of a way of understanding things. Truth is more or less "adequate" in terms of the way it illumines our situation. This adequacy is never perfect, since what is talked about in reference to any particular truth is never fully manifest for what it is. Thus, an empirical notion of truth, in which the "facts" correspond to "reality" is not only mistaken in its supposition that perfect adequacy is possible but presupposes the awareness of reality which is properly called *aletheia*. Even if *aletheia* is never perfectly adequate, however, it is always the ground of any experience of reality. Truth is always present to some extent. Between a minimum and a maximum degree of *aletheia* stands a family resemblance of a plurality of truths which have an infinite potential for being integrated into higher unities. All truths aim at a higher, ultimate oneness, which is approached dialectically as the various domains of truth enter into relations of conflict, harmony, and integration.

Summary and Critical Conclusion

This brief and cursory description of Macquarrie's Heideggerian notion of truth as *aletheia* can be used to introduce the reader to the fundamental problem of this dissertation. Though the basic question with which this work deals can be put in a number of ways, the question that more readily surfaces from these remarks may be put in this way: what is the relationship between truth understood in its primordial sense as *aletheia* and the truths that pertain to the various domains of knowledge, such as science, history, and religion?

Macquarrie, of course, clearly indicates that an understanding of truth as *aletheia* is not in competition with the notions of truth with which theorists in the above-mentioned fields are concerned. *Aletheia* is viewed as the "essence" of truth, the "uncoveredness" that pertains to *any* notion of truth. One can pursue the truths of science, history, ethics, etc., in their own right, paying attention to the criteria that are unique for each region of knowledge, as long as whatever truths may be found in each of them are understood as structures of being that become disclosed, or uncovered, as the pursuit of truth shines its intentional and existential light on their dark corners. Our commitments to truth in any field of inquiry are themselves the fundamental structure of human existence which permit the foundational truth of *aletheia* to emerge, so that *aletheia* is the essence of what appears in this context as well as the defining charactierstic of the truth-seeker as "uncoverer". The relationship between uncoverer and uncovered is what is given in the concept of *aletheia*. It represents the essential concept of existentialist thought to which Macquarrie is committed: *aletheia* manifests the basic epistemological relationship between man and world as man uncovered in his role as uncoverer of a world.

As a philosophical epistemology, this understanding of truth avoids both naive realism and arbitrary subjectivism. Realism is avoided because what appears or emerges as truth reflects the existential structure of man, the truth seeker. Arbitrary subjectivism is avoided because this structure is stable, even if only our choice to seek truth makes it so; and it discloses a world in which the discovery of truth is possible. Being reveals itself under a probing search into the fundamental nature of things, while the unique structures of being which pertain to the various domains of knowledge emerge only as the criteria for truth that are particular for each domain are properly exercised. *Aletheia* is not in competition with these domains of knowledge; it is the most fundamental defining characteristic of truth in all domains.

The truths of each domain, however, are quite different from one another. They do not easily bear on each other. The criteria for what counts, e.g., as good or beautiful, cannot define what counts as scientifically correct or true historically. Some truths in different domains, however, seem to be tied more closely together. We have, e.g., been tempted at various times in history to give scientific justification for religious beliefs—and vice-versa.

Religious knowledge seems, more than any other domain of knowledge, to call forth this attempt to find its justification by some sort of relationship to one of the other domains. Plato, eg., locates the highest knowledge with knowledge of the Good and the Beautiful; and he speaks of this knowledge with religious reverance.[22] Some modern theologians explicitly reduce religious knowledge to anthropology and its attending sciences.[23] Others ground religious claims on historical assertions which they believe support them.[24] Still others ground religious knowledge in moral knowledge.[25]

Religious knowledge (and language) has presented something of a problem for Christians as well as serious scholars of other faiths. The problem which this beginning section of a work on Macquarrie's thought already presents is how Macquarrie perceives religious knowledge. Like so many before him, he chooses to seek justification for religious knowledge in what appears *prima facie* to be another domain of knowledge: in this case, existential philosophy. Key to existential philosophy is the concept of truth as *aletheia*; thus, clearly, religious knowledge must involve *aletheia*.

The question which our epistemological critique must raise, then, is how Macquarrie relates *aletheia* to religious knowledge. This section gives us an insight into how, for the sake of consistency, he *ought* to relate the two: religious knowledge should emerge under its appropriate criteria as a disclosure of Being which is couched in God-talk. And my analysis will bear out that this is roughly how Macquarrie does understand this relationship. He could, of course, have fallen into the trap of *reducing* religious knowledge to the fundamental disclosures of *aletheia* which ground all of the other domains of knowledge. But he remains throughout his work more or less true to the insight that *aletheia* emerges in the context of each domain of thought with the character which the project of truth seeking in that domain determines.

I have said that Macquarrie is "more or less" true to this insight. Indeed, at times he moves in the direction of reducing religious knowledge to the fundamental disclosure of *aletheia*. This is especially the case in his discussions of historical events which are essential issues of faith for Christians. There are also unintended departures of similar kinds in other areas of his works, which I will unfold in the course of this work. But these departures are unintentional slips into a reductionism made easy by what seems to be a nearly inherent religious character of *aletheia*. One cannot judge the value of Macquarrie's contribution to philosophical theology on the basis of them.

On a positive note, Macquarrie presents fragments of a theory which he does not fully explicate or develop and which appear to be the final direction in which his theology ought to go. More than anything else, I want in this work to develop his concept of the alethic manifestation of Being in the context of a notion of how this happens in various domains of human knowledge. This involves returning consistently to the question we have already raised in this first section of *aletheia*: how does *aletheia* relate to this or that domain of knowledge? And a response to that question seems to involve already some responsibility to relate religious knowledge to other fields of knowledge, since it shares with them the concept of *aletheia*.

It is this task of interrelationship which I believe Macquarrie would encourage us to follow through, though at times he explicitly fails to pursue this task with what I consider to be a mistaken justification that such interrelating constitutes worthless speculation. If I fault him on this point, it is only to show that this reticence to move freely beyond existentially based symbols by allowing a fruitful interplay between domains of knowledge abuses his legitimate concept of *aletheia* and the existential-ontological knowledge which engenders and is engendered by the ultimate symbols of language.

Notes

1. John Macquarrie, *Martin Heidegger* (London, 1968), pp. 56—57.
2. John Macquarrie, *Thinking About God* (London, 1975), p. 201.
3. John Macquarrie, *Principles of Christian Theology, rev. ed.*, (London, 1977), p. 119.
4. The following exposition of *aletheia* will clarify what this means. Cf., John Macquarrie, *God-Talk: An Examination of the Language and Logic of Theology* (London, 1967), p. 75.
5. Macquarrie, *Thinking About God*, pp. 20—21.
6. Ibid., pp. 17—18.
7. John Macquarrie, *Existentialism* (Middlesex, England, 1972), pp. 137—138.
   Such a characterization of truth leads naturally to the question concerning the role of a "fact" in this understanding of truth. How do we re-integrate what seems to be a legitimate and fruitful understanding of the world in terms of facts into an understanding which is characterized by wideranging concepts of Being? How does a particular fact of a unique situation, together with its causal nexus, get taken up into an understanding of Being?
8. There are many forms of existentialism, and Macquarrie is not eager to demonstrate which is the "true" one. The essential point in all forms of existentialism is that they distinguish between the being of man and the being of objects of nature. Cf., John Macquarrie, *An Existentialist Theology: A Comparison of Heidegger and Bultmann* (London, 1955), pp. 16—17 and *Existentialism*, p. 283.
9. *An Existentialist Theology*, p. 5.
10. *Existentialism*, p. 250.
11. *An Existentialist Theology*, p. 12.

12. Ibid., p. 14.
13. Ibid., p. 8.
14. Ibid., p. 200.
15. Martin Heidegger, *Being and Time* (trans. by John Macquarrie and Edward Robinson) (London, 1962), p. 84.
16. John Macquarrie, *The Scope of Demythologizing: Bultmann and His Critics* (London, 1960), p. 149.
17. *The Scope of Demythologizing*, p. 149 and *An Existentialist Theology*, pp. 61—62.
18. *The Scope of Demythologizing*, p. 32.

Macquarrie notes that understanding is far more than what we ordinarily take it to be. It cannot be identified with reflection, calculation, thought, etc. It is grounded in what is generally non-reflective in man: mood. Macquarrie says that man is disclosed to himself through mood or "affective state" (*Befindlichkeit*), which has its own form of understanding. Indeed, it is the medium in which a comprehension of being-in-the-world takes place (*An Existentialist Theology*, p. 67).

Moods, or affective states, are intentional: they refer to some state of affairs outside themselves. Hence, they are not simply subjective emotions. The reason that they have been mistaken for subjective states of consciousness which have no bearing on reality is that they generally fail to demonstrate a correspondence between themselves and the presence of certain objects they were supposed to refer to in the world. Instead, however, Macquarrie says that moods are objective in the sense that they refer to situations in which the person participates and knows from within. An analysis of our affective states reveals the way in which we structure the basic situation so that we find a world there for us at all, prior to the development of a theoretical structure that distinguishes between what is objective and what is subjective (*Principles*, p. 98).

Moods most often manifest themselves not in what we think but in how we feel. Feelings are not just "in my mind"; they are correlated with situations or events in the world and are intentional: i.e., they are responses and actions or movements taken in regard to what reveals itself as our world. They are the "mode" in which we "tune in" to the world and participate in situations (*Existentialism*, pp. 161—163).

In this context, we can understand Macquarrie's interpretation of Schleiermacher, who he says maintained an essential unity of feeling and thought toward the end of his life. A fair statement would be that he sought to find in feeling a "leap" by which our thinking transcends all particular objects of thought and reaches towards an all-embracing unity reflected in these particulars and towards which man is directed in the depth of his being. Macquarrie believes he is in consonance with Schleiermacher here and is willing to agree with at least the spirit of his belief that the deepest speculative thoughts are one with the most intimate religious sensations (*Thinking About God*, pp. 161—162). The sort of "feeling" to which both Schleiermacher and Macquarrie are referring here is best expressed by the term "intuition". The "absolute" of Schleiermacher and of Macquarrie's notion of Being are not conceptually grasped but are intuited in an indirect way through feeling (Ibid., 163). Macquarrie would not identify the fundamental feeling as that of "absolute dependance", but he would say that our intuition reaches out toward the facticity (the "hard" reality of objects) and the mystery of existence; hence, he would place himself in this respect in the tradition of Schleiermacher (Ibid., p. 164). No rigid lines can be drawn between the cognitive and the conative, or affective, aspects of man's being. Thus, meaning, the *sense* we uncover in Being, is not just an intellectual construction but is existential and concerns the whole person (Ibid., p. 80).

We should be careful, however, not to conclude that Macquarrie believes feelings are a sure guide to truth. Feelings do intend, or have as their object, a situation in which we are engaged. But what they disclose about it may represent a failure to recognize adequately the character of a situation. Or, they may bury it, misplace it, or put it in the place of another kind of situation. In short, we cannot accept what seems to be the disclosure of a particular situation merely on the grounds of feeling. We need *criteria* for sifting and criticizing the feelings (John Macquarrie, *Studies in Christian Existentialism* (London, 1966), pp. 39—40). While Macquarrie may be an intuitionist in respect to knowledge of human existence and the dynamic structure of Being, he is not merely an intuitionist in respect to other areas of knowledge, such as the sciences, where the empirical approach has its validity. And this latter approach is applicable to the social sciences.

Macquarrie's refusal to separate absolutely the cognitive aspects of thought and feeling is even more strongly stated in his criticism of A.J. Ayer's thought. Macquarrie does not follow A.J. Ayer (Cf., A.J. Ayer, *Language, Truth, and Logic* (New York, 1946) in assering such a separation and locating "truth" only in empirical thought. By arguing that religion is emotive and science is empirical, Ayer tried to erase any contradiction between them. But "truth" was located in science, so that the lack of contradiction here meant only that religion could not be said to consist of meaningful statements which could be true or false. Macquarrie argues, however, that the elimination of the feeling element from religious knowledge leads to the mistaken belief that religious knowledge is reducible to feeling without cognitive content (the emotive theory to which he believes Ayer ascribes). Against this, Macquarrie asserts that our moral and religious feelings, however specific they may be, include affective states that are intentional, carrying with them an awareness, no matter how vague, of our situation in the world. Thus, the "emotions" of emotivism themselves imply a profound awareness of the world which science tries to comprehend, inadequately, with an emotivist theory (*Studies in Christian Existentialism*, pp. 33—34).

Macquarrie reserves some criticism in this vein concerning Ayer's own way of proposing an emotivist theory. Ayer claims that religion is emotive and science is empirical, so that there can be no contradiction between them. But he goes on to say that *science* encroaches upon and *contradicts the feeling of religion* by reducing man's sense of dependence and limitation through technological advancement. Obviously, such an assertion implies that the *assumption* of the religious feeling, namely that man is limited and dependant, is contradicted by the assertions of science; but such a statement should not be possible for Ayer since only empirical assertions can be in contradictory relationship, according to Ayer's own logic. Ayer ends up asserting the notion that religion is not "mere feeling" (*Christ. Ex,* p. 38).

Macquarrie further believes that emotive theories arise from a prejudice about the priority of the physical as an epistemological model and from inadequate views of the structure of discourse which fail to recognize how the disclosure of Being in affective states can be brought to cognitive explicitness (*God-Talk*, p. 82). He agrees with Sir David Ross (*The Foundation of Ethics* (London, 1939), p. 34) that disapproving, considered merely as an "emotive" act, is possible only by *thinking* that what one disapproves of is *worthy of disapproval* (*Christian Existentialism*,

p. 34). Thus, the theory of emotivism reduces itself to the affirmation of what it wishes to deny: that some form of cognition is always a part of feeling, no matter how seemingly far from any kind of thought a feeling may be. And Macquarrie asserts that such cognition implies a grasp of Being, even if only on the lowest level.

Finally, Macquarrie denies the emotivist presupposition that values and commitments block the perception of "pure, intellectual truth". We should note on the contrary that a commitment to the *value* of intellectual honesty and truth is the *sine qua non* of any attainment of truth. The unveiling of truth in any area involves this moral obligation. Further, one does not need to exclude through some sort of "thorough" bracketing one's personal feelings and prejudices in order to produce a reasonably "value-free" science. A commitment to see the given mitigates such influences. One simply subjects his own prejudices to the evidences and subordinates his desires and pleasures to the pursuit of the truth he is seeking. This attitude pertains to all areas of knowledge, including science and theology (John Macquarrie, *Paths in Spirituality* (London, 1967), pp. 64—65).

We are not, however, free to speculatively propose any hypothesis whenever the evidence is not sufficient. Macquarrie says, eg., that existential philosophy is only a mistake if it makes us read into the New Testament thoughts that were not in the minds of the men who wrote it (*Existentialist Theology*, p. 15). The existential analytic, as a phenomenological description of man's own understanding of his being, leads to the border of religious thought even if it doesn't enter religion itself (*ibid*., p. 74). And to press beyond this border by speculation is to err. Existentialism is a philosophy which underlies other areas of knowledge, grounding them in a profound grasp of the Being each area attempts to explicate in its own way. It does not itself yield proofs of assertions in any particular domain of knowledge. We can view Macquarrie's phenomenological ontology as an effort to discern the ontological structure that underlies the world disclosed in the particular domains of knowledge.

19. *Thinking About God*, pp. 16-17. Cf., Ludwig Wittgenstein's *Philosophical Investigations*, Third ed. (U.S., 1969), pp. 66—67, for an insightful presentation of "family resemblances".
20. John Macquarrie, *In Search of Humanity: A Theological and Philosophical Approach* (New York, 1983), p. 63.
21. John Macquarrie, *Christian Unity and Christian Diversity* (London, 1975), p. 34.
22. *The Republic of Plato*, trans. by F. M. Cornford (London, 1945), pp. 211—220 and 231—235.
23. Macquarrie mentions Buri, Bonhoeffer, and Jaspers.
24. One might include here fundamentalists, Biblicists, *et alia*.
25. Cf., Immanuel Kant's *Religion Within the Limits of Reason Alone*.

Degrees of Truth

We have seen that John Macquarrie has a well-developed theory of truth. Having defined his basic concept of truth as *Aletheia*, we can now examine the general means by which we arrive at truth and the degrees with which it is present.

Although Macquarrie is strongly influenced by the existentialist tradition, he is not a proponent of the anti-intellectualism which often accompanies an existentialist orientation. Instead, he views human existence as involving a drive to know. And here he stands firmly in the tradition of Aristotle and Aquinas: all men by nature desire to know.[1] Macquarrie places this desire alongside the desires represented in the variety of our practical concerns on the most fundamental level of human life.[2]

The desire to know does not always produce intellectual knowledge. There is a level or degree of knowing (or *aletheia*) which is not essentially intellectual, but it is, nonetheless, knowledge: the understanding we have of the world in the matrix of our practical concerns. The practical understanding we have of the world as *zuhanden*, the world of concern which we find "ready to hand" in daily life, is our normal, everyday understanding of the world. And it is a "primary" or "first" degree of the revelation of Being. Our most intimate knowledge of the world is the practical "know-how" of finding our way about in the instrumental complex we experience as our immediately given world.[3] Macquarrie says that this "first" level of thinking (hence, of *aletheia*) is concerned with the practical world in the sense of being a calculative mode of thought. Here our thinking is directed toward handling, using, manipulating, etc., the materials of our practical world. We make the world into an "Object" which we "handle" for the satisfaction of our basic human needs. The product of such thought, which is not yet truly reflective, is technology.[4]

Technological thought, however, has a built-in limitation. Our life in the practical world of everyday concerns does not achieve any sense of completion or satisfaction when we pay attention only to such concerns and think only on the level required to solve problems that present themselves in the context of such concerns. The question, "Who am I?" must arise in the context of a world in which, despite our technological advancement, we feel strangely ill at ease. This malaise is grounded in the fact that we cannot stand outside of existence in order to get a detached, synoptic view which would give us a knowledge of the meaning of it all. We are "inside" existence and sense that we are responsible for our being in a way that makes the question of our being, a question to which there is no final, solid answer and which nonetheless cannot be put aside, an essential part of our being.[5] Being becomes an issue for us, an issue that rises out of our existential malaise and anxiety. And these are themselves grounded in our experience of the nothingness which we sense threatens us.[6] Thus, even if we explicitly formulated an intent to live a day to day existence with reference only to the material concerns of the day, we would soon fall into situations and awarenesses which would render this intent impossible to fulfil. For we would begin to search for an understanding which transcends the knowledge gained through calculative thought: we would be forced to seek an understanding of Being which comes only through reflection upon ourselves as thinkers and as existing human beings.[7]

When we question who we are, we move from a focus on what we are doing, on the field of our practical concerns, to a focus on what we *are*. Being rather than the normal world of our activities is revealed in its fundamental characteristics only by means of this reflective shift of focus. For here we cease thinking calculatively and move to a "second" level of thought in which we no longer reduce what is thought about to an "Object" which is opposed to a thinking subject. Here the object is recognized as having the same kind of being as the person who does the thinking. We see ourselves as "participating" in Being with the object of our thought. Being is the common link of participation between what is only later, by an act of reflection, designated as "subject" and "object".

The thought that grasps the thinker's participation in Being is a "second level" of thought which does not make its object, Being, an object at all in the sense of being a scientific object. It is not, in this sense, a "fact".[8] Macquarrie calls this kind of thinking "existential thinking" and asserts that it is a personal act of knowing in which one has access to the *aletheia* of Being in so far as he lets *himself* be disclosed.[9]

Self-knowledge, knowledge of others, and any object of thought that is disclosed through a participation in Being (i.e., through reflective, existential awareness) are all examples of what Macquarrie calls "existential knowledge". Fundamentally, existential knowledge is knowledge gained about Being through the *aletheia* or disclosure that comes as a result of reflection upon human existence. Here we cease our immediate, unreflective, calculative engagement in the world and reflect upon those aspects of Being which are the ground for such engagement. We reflect upon ourselves as actors, thinkers, persons in engagement in order to understand what remains incomprehensible on the level of scientific and practical life. Existential knowledge involves not just observation but interaction and mutual give and take.[10]

Practical-scientific thinking and existential thinking constitute the first two degrees of *aletheia*. The third can be described as ". . . one in which I am subjected to that which is known, one in which I am transcended, mastered, and, indeed, known myself".[11] Following Heidegger, Macquarrie calls this third level "primordial" or essential thinking. In *Was Ist Metaphysik*, Heidegger says this thinking has a meditative character.[12] It is a "waiting" and "listening", a thinking which responds to the address of Being. It is analogous to deeper forms of philosophical, religious, and poetic forms of knowledge and is a paradigm for understanding what is meant by "revelation".[13] Here is our deepest grasp of Being as *aletheia*, a grasp of Being in the most profound way that it "gives" itself.

Primordial thinking gives access to a knowledge of Being that has a giftlike character. In this sense, it is called "revelation". We are *nearly* passive in such thinking, except for our active appropriation[14] of such knowledge. We are not simply overwhelmed by it but receive it through its own power to give itself through what Macquarrie terms "grace": ". . . being gives itself and opens itself, so that we stand in the grace and openness of being. It reveals itself not only in otherness but also in kinship, so that even as we are grasped by it, we can to some extent grasp it in turn and hold to it".[15] This self-giving of Being is the "*fascinans*" of Rudolph Otto's *Mysterium Tremendum et Fascinans*.[16] It is not the product of man's thought but, giving itself only in fragments, is always understood as more vast than one's thoughts. Our own investigations, our own way of putting the question of Being, does not determine the shape and form of the answer, as is the case in practical and existential thinking. It serves instead to excite wonder about Being, a wonder which opens us to its self-giving.[17] This sense of wonder reveals Being as "incomparable" and mysterious. We comprehend it as more "being-ful" than the entities of everyday life and find ourselves standing out from such entities and existing with a renewed awareness of Being. Being stands disclosed: it is *aletheia* itself. As such, it is the *transcendens* pure and simple, which we must try to hear as it gives itself. We submit to it rather than use it to form our own thoughts, ideas, and theories.[18]

This third level of knowledge of Being does not exclude some way of reflecting Being in language. The question concerning the relation between language and being cannot be fully considered here, but we can note in passing at least one way in which this level of *aletheia* or revelation can be expressed: Macquarrie says that the words "being", "is", and "exists" are applied in their various ways in ordinary language by way of analogy, or *analogia entis*. Here we see the influence of the Thomistic tradition on Macquarrie. The general ground for any possible symbolizing of Being by beings such as man must be some kind of *analogia entis*. Being and beings cannot be assimilated one to the other: but they still are inseparable, since Being lets beings be and is present and manifest in them in such a way that, without beings, Being would be indistinguishable from nothingness.[19] Macquarrie would not agree, however, that he is moving away from a Heideggerian form of existentialism in saying this. For this concept of analogy is firmly grounded in what he thinks the later Heidegger means by the "elucidation of being":

> As Heidegger thinks of it, Being is indeed distinct from becoming, but includes becoming, and thus is not a static, eternal Being, but has to be thought of in terms of the temporal horizon, likewise. Being is distinct from appearance, yet is nothing apart from what appears, and so is not some 'thing-in-itself' lurking behind the phenomena. And perhaps this is as far as one can go in the elucidation of the meaning of Being.[20]

We have access through analogies drawn from temporal, changing, realities to the *unitive* nature of Being as experiences in its "alethic" self-givingness. We can finally speculate (using analogical devices) that Being, though stable and unitive in itself, is pouring itself out in terms of time or becoming in such a direction that all things move toward being gathered up again into a unity. Here we see that Being is not static and frozen but is stable by being a constant process of gathering itself up as a unity. We have touched the Christian concept of a God who creates beings which move toward being gathered up into a unity with God and with each other to dwell in a state of being in which new vistas of crativity reveal themselves.[21]

This use of analogy does not yield philosophical proofs. This understanding of Being is, according to Macquarrie, a speculative one. We must note in passing that Macquarrie does view this "vision of God" as speculative, for we will wish to raise the issue in another section, whether this sort of speculation is an example of the sort that ought to play a role in theology.

We are able at this point, however, to see that, for Macquarrie, the process of appropriating truth is successful in degrees. Thus, we can say that there are degrees of truth. And these degrees are measured in terms of their *adequacy*, their success in lighting up what is spoken about. Our discourse is true when it adequately performs its function of letting us *see*. Again we find the influence of the Thomistic tradition on Macquarrie, for the idea of adequation is central to Aquinas' conception of truth as *adaequatio intellectus et rei*, though Macquarrie understands *adaequatio* somewhat differently.[22] Whereas Aquinas understood *adaequatio intellectus et rei* as a "correspondence" of thought and reality, Macquarrie understands it as a "degree of light" or illumination of our situation: i.e., the disclosure of a world which precedes any distinction between an idea of a thing and the thing itself. Thus, "adequacy" does not depend upon conceptual pictures which are supposed to "mirror" reality. Indeed, such pictures can obscure the truth when we attend *to* them rather than *through* them toward what they are trying to represent.[23]

Truth, then, may be evalutated according to degrees of adequacy, degrees which refer to the clarity and depth of the disclosure of the human situation, which includes all systems of understanding. Especially in regard to theology, "adequacy" means that no degree of truth or clarity is wholly adequate; nor is any statement completely devoid of truth. We can *always* pursue truth in the interest of gaining a greater degree of adequacy, which becomes, when achieved, a foundation of yet deeper discoveries.[24] A secondary understanding of truth to which Macquarrie seems committed is the concept of the "horizon" of adequacy: "the truth". In reference to this horizon, he says, ". . . truth is the ideal or limiting case, in which that which is talked about has been fully manifested for what it is".[25] And if this ideal limit is unobtainable, we must recognize in humility that this is so not only because we do not have all of the answers, but also because we do not have all of the questions. Our lack of knowledge, of complete adequacy, is simply part of what it means not to be God, to be finite.[26]

Summary

These sections on truth and its degrees have attempted to clarify Macquarrie's notion of *aletheia*. Grounded deeply in the thought of Martin Heidegger, Macquarrie's concept of truth is intimately informed by themes of existentialism. Truth is *aletheia*, or "unconcealment". As such, it is an event that takes place in the human person, an event in which the person trusts, commits himself, and lives in terms of a way of understanding things. Truth is more or less "adequate" in terms of the way it illumines our situation, the way in which it discloses not only the nature of the world but also we who live in it and seek the deeper meanings of it.

There are three levels of knowledge of Being as *aletheia*. The first is the practical understanding we have of it in the concerns of everyday life, in which we distinguish readily between "subject" (knower) and "Object" (known). This is the level of calculative thought. But this level does not answer the inescapable question: Who am I? We want to know ourselves and reality in respect to the Being that we are vaguely aware surrounds us, bordered by a sense of nothingness that makes us feel ill at ease in the world. Our reflection upon the Being that pertains to both reality (object) and myself (subject), that links us in an indefinable commonality, is a second level of knowledge of Being. It is a second level of *aletheia*. Here we see ourselves as participating as beings in the Being that is known. This is existential thinking, since one thinks oneself as participating in Being while, in the act of thinking, still stands outside of Being (ex-isting). Yet this participation does give us access to being in such way that we can begin to speak of being itself, if only by analogical language. Our transcendence of the categories of nature and of human existence in our understanding of being, our attempt to express Being in creative, new syntheses informed by analogical language, constitutes a third level of truth, "essential" or "primordial" thinking.

No level of truth is ever wholly adequate. Thus, an empirical notion of truth in which the "facts" correspond to "reality" is not only mistaken in its supposition that perfect adequacy is possible but presupposes the awareness of reality which is properly called *aletheia*. Even if *aletheia* is never perfectly adequate, however, it is always the ground of any experience of reality. Truth is always present to some extent. Between a minimum and a maximum degree of *aletheia* stands a family resemblance of a plurality of truths which have an infinite potential for being integrated into higher unities. These higher unities involve an attempt to express something about the nature of Being itself, a task that is never finished but is always on-going.

Notes

1. Cf., *Aristotle's Metaphysics* (Trans. by Richard Hope) (Ann Arbor, 1966), p. 3.
2. John Macquarrie, *Existentialism* (Middlesex, England, 1972), p. 89.
3. John Macquarrie, *An Existentialist Theology: A Comparison of Heidegger and Bultmann* (London, 1955), pp. 55—56. Perception is a mode of knowing, but it is considered less intimate than practical "know-how" knowledge. Of course, theoretical knowledge, such as that constituting the sciences, is less intimate than this degree of *aletheia*.
4. John Macquarrie, *Principles of Christian Theology* (London, 1977), p. 91.
5. John Macquarrie, *Studies in Christian Existentialism* (London, 1966), pp. 6—7.
6. *Principles*, p. 107. Macquarrie is following Heidegger quite closely here. Heidegger understands anxiety as a flight in the face of death, which is our existential encounter with nothingness.
7. John Macquarrie, *New Directions in Theology Today: Vol. III: God and Secularity* (London, 1968), p. 16.
8. *Principles*, p. 92.
9. Ibid., pp. 92—93.
10. *Existentialism*, p. 134. We shall find that even faith in God is a form of existential thinking for Macquarrie.
11. *Principles*, p. 94.
12. Cf., Martin Heidegger's *Was ist Metaphysik*, pp. 47—49.
13. *Principles,* p. 94.
14. "Appropriation" = "taking to oneself", "living in terms of".
15. *Principles*, p. 95.
16. Rudolph Otto, *The Idea of the Holy* (trans. by John W. Harvey) (London, 1971), pp. 8—41. Cf., *Principles*, p. 95.
17. *Studies in Christian Existentialism*, p. 92.
18. Ibid., pp. 88—92.
19. *Principles*, p. 138.
20. John Macquarrie, *Martin Heidegger* (London, 1968), p. 50.
21. *Principles,* pp. 358—359.
22. John Macquarrie, *God-Talk: An Examination of the Language and Logic of Theology* (London, 1967), pp. 75—76.

23. John Macquarrie, *Thinking About God* (London, 1975), pp. 23—24. Such a dynamic is especially troublesome in theology when we are trapped in a religious faith that relies on literalism and is unable to convey the deeper religious truths toward which our literal concepts point.
24. Ibid., p. 26.
25. *God-Talk*, p. 26.
26. John Macquarrie, *Twentieth-Century Religious Thought: The Frontiers of Philosophy and Theology, 1900—1960* (London, 1963), p. 372.

Science

The heart of this dissertation centers around the issue concerning whether facts are important in the Christian faith and whether speculation concerning them plays a proper role in theology. One would suppose that facts are important to Christian faith since Christians make important historical claims and sometimes important scientific claims (eg., the assertion of creationism). Thus, one has a *prima facie* reason to suppose that scientific thinking and all other modes of thinking which concern themselves with facts are essential to a Christian philosophy.

But I have found it difficult to discover just what role Macquarrie ascribes to facts in the development of his Christian philosophy. Indeed, if we understand a "fact" fundamentally to be a judgment concerning what is—or was—the case in the world, we often find Macquarrie speaking as if the truth were something *other* than the facts. And this "otherness" appears at times to be a negative otherness in the sense that facts and the methodologies that establish them are "by-passed" or considered irrelevant in the establishment of a more profound existential or ontological truth. Indeed, the *aletheia* of "essential" thinking is expressed in language which does not consider itself factual, though it considers itself more true (or adequate for the discursive expression of Being) for this very reason: it *transcends* the specific events in which Being is ordinarily experienced and expressed in everyday practical concerns and in scientific-calculative thinking, aiming instead at essential insights into Being.

Macquarrie's view of truth as comprising three levels of *aletheia* which are hierarchically ordered in their value of adequacy poses a paradox for the Christian thinker: How can we value essential thinking as the highest grasp of Being—or God—when the facts of the events of Jesus' historical reality, especially the resurrection, are considered as a factual (or "first") level of knowledge, ultimately irrelevant in the establishment of an essential insight into Being? We will see that Macquarrie does not find it necessary to "speculate" on the nature of these facts beyond the consideration of their *possibility*. What actually happened on Easter Day is not nearly so important as the insight into Being which the mere possibility of the resurrection adequately communicates; and this insight, grasped through the dynamic of a faith that *something* happened, seems to make any further pursuance of historical or relevant scientific truth a moot question. Such projects are termed "speculation" in the sense that any conclusion would remain ungrounded. The "facts" which seemed *prima facie* to be essential to Christian faith seem now to have paled so much before the more profound disclosures of Being of which they were the supposed medium that they have no essential role to play in the *aletheia* theology seeks to discover.

How do the essential, truth-mediating facts get lost in Macquarrie's philosophical theology? *Must* they be lost, or do the facts, both historical and scientific, play an *essential* role in the on-going projects of Christian thought? Even if Macquarrie has allowed the facts to lose their significance in Christian thinking, does theology demand this loss? Or is Macquarrie mistaken in taking this direction? These are the questions which are at the heart of this inquiry. We will find, I believe, that Macquarrie's thought does tend toward a "fact-denying" ontology; but we will also find not only that this direction is unnecessary and constitutes a wrong turn in theology but that Macquarrie himself does not seriously intend such a turn—and provides within the substance if not the intention of his writings adequate ways of dealing with the paradox I have posed.

We can begin an analysis of this paradoxical relationship between knowledge of the facts and knowledge of Being (or the second and third levels of *aletheia*) by examining the nature of a fact as we generally understand and encounter it in what Macquarrie understands as essentially constituting the sciences. We will in this section take up his concept of factual knowledge, including science and history, and then move to an analysis of existential-ontological knowledge, which includes his use of phenomenology and the consequent ontology it implies. Finally, in the context of a discussion of his concept of language, we can move to an analysis of symbols and analogy, which constitute the third level of *aletheia*.

The first level of knowledge involves an "objective content" which allows us to operate both physically and intellectually in the physical world. This level includes not only the immediate life of physical and emotional engagement in the world but also the calculative-technological knowledge constituting the sciences. It is in the sciences that the facts are posited as "objective". On this level of knowledge, facts are "true statements" (i.e., they state what is the case in the world), and reason has their establishment as its aim.

We must at this point distinguish Macquarrie's philosophy of science from that of other philosophers. For such an analysis is necessary in order to determine more clearly what Macquarrie means by a "fact".

Macquarrie eschews the strict criteria of logic and mathematics as defining the scope of reason. But although he would not make logic or mathematics the model of what counts as rationality, he asserts that we cannot let reason slip in order to follow an intensity of experience and passion.[1] Reason must be active in the pursuit of knowledge. Our knowledge-claims must be *reasonable*. And this is minimally defined as a claim which does not depend for its acceptance upon a belief or argument that is unacceptable to reason.

But the formal criteria for validity, the "objective" fashion in which logic and mathematics establish their propositions, cannot be the sole model for "reasonableness". For we rarely ever consider an idea to be reasonable only when it is the implication (in the strict, logical sense) of other ideas we hold to be true. Generally we use a looser criterion for "reasonableness": we consider as reasonable any idea which does not offend against reason, understood as a total complex of commonly understood ideas which do not themselves stand in any logically contradictory relationship. Macquarrie seems to adopt this "looser" role or reason in his philosophy of science.

Macquarrie sees no need to "hold out" on assigning a truth value to a claim until "all" the evidence is in, until all were "finished or complete". We can never have an objective viewpoint "outside" of the truth we are seeking to know, so that we can judge the agreement or disagreement between thought and our knowledge-claim. Macquarrie asserts that such a vantage point could never be achieved; so we cannot identify truth with the *ideal* of objectivity that we encounter in scientific thinking.[2] Knowledge in general, especially that gained in the sciences, involves learning how to think, observe, conjecture, engage in critical discussion, etc.; and this is possible only in a community of learning, a tradition, which not only preserves a body of objective knowledge but generates a living, continuing succession of teachers and learners.[3] Scientific knowledge is a living, ongoing process, not a "finished result". We cannot and need not attain perfect objectivity.

Macquarrie's concept of the existential situation in knowing throws light on the distinction between subjectivity and objectivity as a determinant of truth in the sciences. Since both terms are an abstraction of the concept of being-in-the-world,[4] the ideal of objectivity cannot be separated from the "subjective" process of coming to know in the context of an ambiguous world of meanings. Thus, an understanding of nature does not begin with nature but with an existential self-understanding of our way of being as a part of nature. And this results in a "total" concept of being-in-the-world: nature.[5] We will return to this existential aspect of scientific knowledge later, only pausing here to note that Macquarrie views it as presupposed in all scientific knowing. "Nature", then, is primordially grasped in the unified context of our situation as "total" (thinking, feeling, believing, etc.) persons.[6]

But this is not the nature we encounter in the sciences. For we can "dim down" whatever belongs to the self as "personal" being (feeling, volition, value-judgments, concern, etc.) so that the self remains only as a mere cognitive point or subject which stands over against its object. Here the participant is reduced to being an observer. He speaks only of "objective" facts, which are abstractions from a total context of existence. We must be able to perform such acts, of course, in order to concentrate on and organize our knowledge of the world; only then can we predict and manage the phenomena composing it. But the problem with doing this is that one can take this "objective" view of reality to be the model for understanding all of reality, and this belief leads to positivism. And this distorted view cannot reasonably be raised up as a paradigmatic expression of knowledge.[7] Our view of nature and of the process by which we come to understand it must incorporate the existential thinking that is at the base of all forms of understanding in every field of knowledge, even if the specific project of science does have its own process of conceptualization.

Macquarrie, then, is prepared to reject scientific positivism as a scientific methodology, not because it has no validity as a methodology, but because it tries to claim too much for itself as a means of understanding reality as a whole. In respect of this claim, Macquarrie agrees with the familiar criticism that the verificationist principle that is at the root of positivism cannot itself be understood as "true" within positivism since it is neither a tautology nor an empirically verifiable proposition.[8] Agreeing with John Wisdom, he notes that the verificationist principle is exactly what it claims no principle should be: a metaphysical principle—and a "smashing" one![9] Because it assumes a metaphysical function in organizing our knowledge claims, it arrogates to itself the right to judge religious, ethical, and aesthetic claims according to its own criteria, thus effecting a reductionism of these to "emotive" experiences which carry no conceptual weight.[10]

Macquarrie is more receptive to Karl Popper's falsifiability theory as a way of approaching scientific knowledge.[11] This approach understands scientific knowledge as the fruit of an attempt to falsify existing theories rather than to verify hypotheses. He agrees with Popper's criticism of Ayer that the process of verification can easily involve an interpretation of the data which tends to confirm theories we want to believe in. And one of the attractions of this approach for Macquarrie is that falsifiability theory has never been able to falsify the claims of Christianity. He notes that Anthony Flew has shown that Christianity is unscientific, but he does not take this demonstration to be fatal to the use of falsifiability theory, since he does not believe that Christianity must be scientific,[12] even if he doesn't believe it should *oppose* science. The reason for this is that science and religion each stem from different projects of understanding, the former from theoretical projects aimed at understanding nature, and the latter from a more inclusive existential project aimed at understanding reality as a whole. Conflict arises only when one of those projects claims to be the only proper means of understanding anything.[13]

Some questions, then, should be treated as scientific ones, whereas others are to be viewed as religious questions which require a different approach.[14] Some important questions which may *seem* to be religious or which are scientific but have import for religious thought must be approached as scientific questions. The origin of the universe, for example, is a scientific question, as are questions about the ultimate destiny of the universe. Human history represents too brief an episode in time to say anything about the ultimate end of history based on what we know, and *theological assertions may be contradicted by the facts*,[15] where the "facts" are defined as conditions of reality uncovered by a scientific method.[16]

Macquarrie is distinguishing here between facts and other kinds of knowledge: religious, historical, and, we must suppose, other knowledge-claims in the various domains of human experience besides that represented by the sciences. And he makes the very suggestive remark, which we must later follow up on more fully, that the facts can *contradict* theological and, by implication, perhaps other assertions. He does not clarify here how knowledge-claims grounded in radically different projects can be placed in a linguistic frame of reference which provides the seemingly necessary common ground for contradiction to be possible. And he does not develop any clear notion concerning whether these contradictions might be *correctives* leading to broader and more fruitful views.

Macquarrie's claim that facts can contradict religious assertions does not seem to be consistent with the apparent aim of his distinction between religious and scientific truth: to make at least some important religious assertions properly impervious to judgment according to scientific criteria, and some important scientific truths impervious to judgment according to scientific criteria, and some important scientific truths impervious to judgment according to religious criteria. This aim seems to be a correct one, and Macquarrie's point is well-taken. But we must insist on preserving the truth which Macquarrie has let slip here as a kind of unintending afterthought: some theological assertions can be contradicted by the facts. We must assume that he intends to include as vulnerable to contradiction factual assertions we might like to make because of our commitment to certain religious notions (which, we might add, cannot themselves be considered "facts"). But if this sensible supposition is correct, then he includes such assertions under the rubric of theology. And this means there can be facts that pertain so strongly to a religious mode of knowing that they can legitimately be referred to as "religious facts" or theological facts. But this is precisely the notion he intends to avoid in order to maintain the aim of his distinction between science and religion. If this sensible supposition is, however, incorrect,. then it becomes very difficult to know what he means by "contradiction" or the distinction between science and religion. In sum, I am pointing to a fruitful notion which I will term "crossreferencing corrective", which accidentally underlies Macquarrie's intention to distinguish sharply between science and religion. And I will later develop this notion to overcome some of the problems which Macquarrie's existential theology poses.

According to the main intent of Macquarrie's analysis, then, Christian thought does not set itself up as a judge concerning what can be true or false in science. It views the physical universe as a visible expression of a deeper reality which has affinity with man in his personal and spiritual being, a reality which supports and values peace and wholeness. Man is viewed as a "co-worker" in this context, a co-creator of peace, which is the primordial reality at which the universe aims.[17] Nature is a *context* in which we live, a context having its own being which must be discovered through a scientific approach to it. In this sense, Macquarrie says that philosophy should never seek to vaunt a humanism over its responsibility to deal with the facts which science yields.[18]

But what does it mean to say that "peace and wholeness" are the primordial realities at which nature aims, except that these are the *direction* in which nature moves? But nature is always in process, always becoming something other than what it is. And science is still called upon to study these processes (chemical reactions, biological transformations, growth and decay, etc.). Why is the movement toward peace and wholeness different? One cannot naively suppose, of course, that calling them "realities" means that they are facts which can be studied by scientific methodologies. But one cannot suppose either that these realities and scientific facts are radically and ontologically disconnected. For Christians wish to speak of events in the world which science has as its object, events which could be experienced not only inwardly but also as "objective" events. Christianity demands this reference to the *same* reality which science observes, studies, and attempts to explain; for it wishes to declare that reality itself is a party to God's redemptive activity. Thus, Christian faith cannot be reduced to the "meaning" or interpretation of the facts. This would render the Christian's claim meaningless. So the world which science studies is "wrapped up" in the primordial realities which the Christian says nature aims at. And any project which aims at clarifying the primordial realities which are viewed from within the domain of religion as grounded in God must *somehow* affect the project of the sciences. For the project of "faith-interpretation" must speak in reference to the world science takes as real. That is why a scientific fact can contradict a theological assertion: Theological assertions imply or presuppose or even sometimes explicitly state that some particular state of affairs is or was the case; and science can disprove this claim. Or, science might also show that such a claim is correct; and such a demonstration may reveal that there is an intimate connection between the theological understanding which produced the scientific claim and the claim itself. That "connection" can be expressed only in a language which either integrates or displays an important interplay between the two projects of faith and science, making each an expressed element of both.[19] Macquarrie, however, does not develop this mutually correcting interplay of science and religious thought toward the more fruitful conception which seems to be required for an understanding of what Christian faith is about in a natural world to which believers are tied.

Macquarrie does say that the scope of scientific thinking has its limitation and that one cannot extent the empirical approach to all areas of knowledge, particularly not to the knowledge of human reality itself. Scientific thinking is useful in the natural sciences but not in other *domains* of knowledge, in so far as they do not pursue factual knowledge. This is particularly true of the narrower empiricism which identifies knowledge with sense experience and verification. But he says that *broader* forms of empiricism would allow talk about interpersonal, moral, aesthetic, and religious experience and are, for that reason, more acceptable.[20]

Macquarrie's rejection of this narrower empiricism as a fundamental philosophy which claims to cover all areas of knowledge can be summed up by the following points:[21]

1) Not all knowledge begins from observation.
2) Conjectures and hypotheses can be more fruitful than inductive generalizations.
3) Critical detachment is a hindrance in developing knowledge, particularly in the study of humanity.
4) Knowledge is a function of an active self-participation in a world and does not consist of data collected by an abstract thinking subject.
5) There is tacit knowledge which cannot ever be fully stated ranging from the skills of craftsmen to the visions of mystics.
6) Knowledge of facts is one kind of knowledge among others, such as knowing people and ourselves.
7) The concept of knowledge is much broader than that of narrow empiricist epistemology.

These criticisms show that although empiricism and the sciences that are grounded in it have their rightful place in human thought, that place is delimited in scope by evidence of forms of knowledge that are distinctly *different* from that of science and by inherent limitations within empiricism itself. Macquarrie believes that our tendency to reduce our world-view to one modeled after science (or positivistic science) is grounded in our tendency to avoid raising fundamental questions of meaning. We prefer to leap from one limited context to another and tend to lapse into a superficial life in which positivism provides an escape from more profound thought.[22]

This is not to decry the achievements of positivistic science. While such science has not introduced new or resolved old philosophical problems, it has adequately destroyed the old naturalism, the mechanistic materialsm of the 19th century, even if it does not point to theism.[23] But Macquarrie's assertion that the limited contexts of meaning which it has produced is an unfortunate development should imply—though Macquarrie himself does not make such a conclusion explicit—that *all* knowledge should be organized in one, interconnected context which provides the profundity in which we can speak of Being, God, and human destiny. This ideal may be unachievable, but one can move in its direction by developing a cross-referencing and mutually corrective interplay among the various domains of knowledge, establishing as a preliminary criterion that what is held to be true in one domain should not explicitly contradict what is held to be true in another, even if paradox and mystery must be given their rightful place. This criterion accords well with Macquarrie's own "looser" acceptance of empiricism as a proper approach in the sciences. But an explicitation of this methodology must await the conclusion of this work. I mention it here only to indicate the direction in which I intend, with legitimate reason based on Macquarrie's own ideas, to take Macquarrie's thought.

Even if Macquarrie does not seem to move in the direction of a developed theory of an interplay of domains, he does attempt to show how the domain of scientific thought is *not incompatible* with religious thought. We may now turn to an explicitation of Macquarrie's own view of science and the nature of the universe it comprehends. This view of science is compatible with other domains of thought because what it asserts about the physical nature of the world does not deny what may be true about it from other perspectives, even if it does not itself delineate the truths that may be discovered in the light of these other perspectives.

Macquarrie acknowledges that other dimensions of thought may have logics of their own[24] and that each of these domains of thought also manifest different degrees of knowing[25] as well as criteria of validity which are appropriate to each one and which may not be applicable to other domains.

Each domain is grounded in empirical evidence,[26] though the empirical evidence for any particular conception, particularly the central and most wide-ranging ones, is never just "raw" data or raw sensation. There is no such thing as "raw" sensation. The raw data of the senses is always grasped as immediately subjected to interpretation; sensation never exists in isolation, but manifests in a context of meaning which is equiprimordial with sensation and is confirmed, disqualified, or transformed in the context of meaning:[27] "Every science, every intellectual discipline, involves its practitioners in a form of spirituality, in valuations, aspirations, and commitments".[28]

The context of meaning in which perception participates is not a static, unchanging context. Ultimately, this context is the entire body of knowledge which has been developed through human history in any particular domain. Knowledge, as well as other aspects of human life and transcendence, develops a tradition with a life of its own. Meaning, present in terms of the entire tradition of interpretation, is always somewhat more than any particular perception or idea. As a result, our affirmations always have more meaning than we intend and are capable of various proper interpretations. And we can always derive more from the tradition than we put into it.[29]

It is in such complex contexts of meaning that the project of science is carried on. The ultimate context of meaning, of course, is the tradition of understanding connected with Being. Particular beings are determinate and particular in so far as they "stand between nothing and being".[30] What science counts as the beings it studies and attempts to comprehend appear as such only in the context of an understanding of Being. Macquarrie seems to understand beings as resisting nothingness so that they leave around them a "space" of nothing which constitutes their determinateness.

Beings are not connected together by a network of totally determining causes. The universe of beings includes randomness, purposiveness, and creativity.[31] Setting aside even the idea of providence that most Christian theologians assert, Macquarrie says there is in the world a randomness which enables some events and material combinations to occur that would not otherwise be present or able to realize their potential.[32] But alongside randomness and chance is the evidence of nature's free, purposive behavior. Randomness and purpose function together to bring nature to a finished and fully realized state, a state which is yet unfinished.[33]

Nature, developing through both chance and purposiveness, shows evidence of being already highly organized. Macquarrie speaks of nature as progressing toward a hierarchical structural organization composed of "higher" and "lower" levels of being which are interdependant and which progressively emerge into higher levels of being. He says, "We seem to be justified in speaking of 'levels' and in distinguishing 'higher' and 'lower' levels (of a hierarchy of beings in nature) because . . . some kinds of being include others, and thus display a wider range of being and a higher unity that embraces a more multiple diversity".[34]

The hierarchy of beings extends from the elemental energies and the physical framework of nature to living organisms and to man. The higher level of being develops from the lower by *emergence*. Emergence is defined as a "leap" from a lower level to a higher. This leap is made possible by a growth of complexity in a lower level that may be gathered up in a new and more comprehensive unity.[35] The *quality* of the new being is different. And, for this reason, it cannot be reduced to a mere concatenation of elements of the lower level. Emergent levels introduce *novel* elements. Our inability to explain novelty by reductionism indicates that the emergent level comes from the hiddenness of Being itself.[36]

Emergence means, then, that the lower level is not merely what its level indicates. Man, for example, is not merely a physical, living organism. His being is indeed a novel unity of material being, living organism, etc. But he is not reducible to these. Emergent unities cannot be explained in terms of factors operative in lower levels alone. The critical moments of emergence produce new levels.[37]

Macquarrie claims that knowledge of the emergent structural organization of nature is gained most readily by beginning phenomenologically with human existence and abstracting down the scale of being. We are not required to deduce this by starting from within nature.[38] Science, like other domains of knowledge, is ultimately grounded in the phenomenological ontology that begins with human existence. But each domain of knowledge, including science, takes on its unique character as this fundamental understanding of Being is carried into widely different human experiences and projects. In all areas of knowledge, the process of emergence is the process of Being's self-communication. Thus, the higher the level in the hierarchy of beings that a being occupies, the widest diversity in unity it can exhibit, since Being is more present and manifest in it.[39] Beings must be understood not only in terms of the elements that make them up, but also "from above down", and this is especially true of man.[40]

The world, then, is one, but it may be interpreted from various standpoints, such as those of science, art, and religion. Each of these different ways of interpreting the world brings forth a different "dimension" or domain of it. And man can continue to discover new dimensions of the world.[41] These dimensions interface with each other in ways which call us constantly to seek more profound unities of truths "between" domains. Macquarrie circumscribes his notion of the relativity of truths within a world of plural dimensions or domains with a higher concept of unity toward which they all move. He says that, though truth is multiform, though there are different kinds of truth for different dimensions of experience, all of which need exploration and clarification concerning the criteria of truth that are proper for each dimension, we need to view these differences as various forms of a higher unity of truth. Even if the structure of this higher unity is not immediately evident, we can, perhaps, discover a "family resemblance" among different kinds of truth.[42] Thus, truth has a unity that is progressively comprehended in the context of its organic connection to our fundamental situation as human beings, and it manifests a progressive deeper unity with other truths that lie outside the domain of any particular truth.

Summary and Conclusion of the Science Section

Science establishes our factual knowledge of the physical world. These facts are not those which are narrowly defined by a positivist epistemology undergirded by a verificationist criterion. Instead, they are the product of what Macquarrie calls a "broader" kind of empiricism which does not confine its notion of experience to "raw sense data" but extends its scope of experiential grounding to the much broader categories of interpersonal, moral, aesthetic, and religious aspects of life. The most functional criterion is that of "reasonableness", so that what is true empirically in one domain of human experience is said not to be in conflict with what is true in another unless its assertion is "unreasonable" in the face of the other; i.e., unless it is an assertion that would seem to be falsified either by its own evidences or by the truths held in other domains.

Macquarrie outlines two ideas that are important for the development of a direction of theological thought which is inherent in his work but which does not receive the attention it warrants. These ideas are found in his concept of the science of nature as one domain of knowledge among others (which are never exhaustively or clearly delineated) and in his notion of the hierarchical interrelationship of entities in nature. The first of these ideas effects a separation between the various domains of human intellectual effort, allowing them each to develop areas of genuine knowledge grounded in regions of experience which are germane to them and governed by criteria that are pertinent and somehow inherent. Thus, one sees that science, history and religion are all generally independent "domains" of thought. One might also suggest that political science and economics among other regions of knowledge, are also independent domains.

The second important idea lies in the notion of an organized hierarchy of being which Macquarrie argues is foundational in physical nature. This idea slides out of science into ontology, but I have presented it under the rubric of a discussion of Macquarrie's concept of the scientific endeavor because he believes it is a scientific ontology, one whose notions give firm ground to the obvious evidence of the interconnections of things in the physical universe and which finds continued confirmation in the discoveries of science. Thus, lower levels of beings form the ground upon which higher levels are dependent and from which they emerge in order, by a combination of movements determined by natural law and free randomicity, to form higher unities of being in which Being is more fully manifest. These higher levels are the potential of the lower levels; and we can understand the nature of the lower levels more fully "from above downward" once the higher has emerged.

Part of the notion of an ordered hierarchy of beings in Macquarrie's scientific ontology seems to be a peculiar parallel between the material hierarchy that is discovered in physical nature and a hierarchy of ideas which forms in the process of discovery. One can say, of course, that it is trivially absurd to note that one's idea about reality end up taking on the same shape as the reality they intend to describe. After all, one might argue, we can't really distinguish between the content of an idea and what the idea describes in physical nature. All we are concerned with as scientists is the *idea* of reality and not ontology. And, as scientists, we might be able to get away with this collapse of the material and ideological orders of being. But Macquarrie is not *just* speaking from (and about) a scientific point of view. He is transcending science in order to show the sort of thinking that makes science possible. He cannot help treading into the area of a more general ontology than science itself affords because one cannot speak in a general way easily at all about the interrelations of beings as discovered in science without saying something about the nature and structure of beings in general. And that seems to involve ontology. And not only does it involve ontology, but, because Macquarrie must distinguish between the ideas that intentionally attain a grasp of reality and the reality they grasp, it also involves a description of how the epistemological process achieves its goal. And here the parallel I spoke of is relevant: less complex and more disordered ideas move, under the impetus of both the inherent potential of idea-forming which their incomplete structures suggest and allow and the free determinations of imagination, toward more complex and "higher" unities of the notion of Being. The *meaning* of Being is more fully manifest in these higher unities, even if these higher concepts are dependant upon the "lower" unities from which they emerge. Just as in the physical order of nature, the higher unities of the comprehension of Being do not have a necessary, determined relation to that which supports them and may appear to have quite a different character from their lower support levels, just as the nature of water differs considerably from that of hydrogen and oxygen.

One important aspect of this latter idea must be noted: the scientific ontology Macquarrie outlines is an idea that emerges from the "lower" concepts functioning within the sciences themselves. The relationship of hierarchical emergence obtains between the sciences and this more general ontology. This suggests already that the first level of *aletheia*, which includes the sciences, is connected to the second, which includes existential and ontological knowledge, in precisely the same way in which the ideas (and entities) within the science of physical nature are connected. Thus, a phenomenological ontology should represent not just "another" level of *aletheia*, but an *emergent* level of knowledge which possesses higher unities of conceptual purchase on the meaning of Being, corresponding to ontological realities which are their intentional object. If this is true, and we must first enter into an analysis of Macquarrie's phenomenology and its resultant ontology before claiming this, then the sciences, the search for factual knowledge in all domains of human knowledge, must be seen as *supporting* this emergence. And the facts they establish must be interpreted in the light of the higher unities of knowledge they support. Thus, an interplay between interpretation and factual claims is set in motion, aiming at the emergence of yet higher unities of knowledge. And this dynamic is what we will later interpret as "inner, tensional cross-referencing". But we must examine Macquarrie's second level of knowledge before being able to give concrete content to this claim and move to this interpretation of the relation between facts and the interpretive context in which they dwell.

Notes

1. John Macquarrie, *Existentialism* (Middlesex, England, 1972), p. 277.
2. John Macquarrie, *Thinking About God* (London, 1975), p. 20.
3. John Macquarrie, *In Search of Humanity: A Theological and Philosophical Approach* (New York, 1983), p. 65. Cf., Michael Polanyi, *The Tacit Dimension* (New York, 1967), pp. 55—92.
4. John Macquarrie, *Studies in Christian Existentialism* (London, 1966), pp. 35—36.
5. John Macquarrie, *Principles of Christian Theology* (London, 1977), p. 222.
6. John Macquarrie, *An Existentialist Theology: A Comparison of Heidegger and Bultmann* (London, 1955), p. 24.
7. John Macquarrie, *God-Talk: An Examination of the Language and Logic of Theology* (London, 1967), 69—70.
8. John Macquarrie, *Twentieth-Century Religious Thought: the Frontiers of Philosophy and Theology, 1900—1960* (London, 1963), p. 315.
9. *God-Talk*, p. 60. Cf., John Wisdom, *Philosophy and Psychoanalysis* (Oxford, 1953), p. 245.
10. *Christian Existentialism*, pp. 32—33.
11. Cf., Karl Popper, *Objective Knowledge* (Oxford, 1972), p. 7.
12. *Humanity*, pp. 62—63. Cf., A. Flew & A. MacIntyre (eds.), *New Essays in Philosophical Theology* (London, 1955), pp. 96, ff.
13. *Existentialist Theology*, p. 64.
14. *Principles*, p. 32; 24—29.
15. John Macquarrie, *The Scope of Demythologizing: Bultmann and his Critics* (London, 1960), p. 61.
16. John Macquarrie, *Paths in Spirituality* (London, 1967), pp. 66—77.
17. John Macquarrie, *The Concept of Peace* (London, 1973), p. 70.
18. *Existentialism*, p. 281.
19. *Christian Existentialism*, p. 27.
20. *Humanity*, pp. 59—60; p. 200. This statement is, however, too weak to indicate a program of corrective integration. Cf., the concluding essay of this work for a discussion of a workable means of relating the different domains of knowledge.
21. Ibid., pp. 67—68.
22. *Thinking About God*, p. 94.
23. *Twentieth-Century Religious Thought*, pp. 250—251.
24. *Existentialism*, p. 143.
25. Ibid., p. 133. Ideas may be, eg., precise or vague, shallow or profound, etc.
26. If Macquarrie means this at all, he means it in the sense of this much broader empiricism which he finds more acceptable than positivism in the sciences. But, even if all domains of knowledge can be said to involve empirical evidence, it is difficult to understand how Macquarrie could maintain that they are *grounded* in empirical

evidence, as though their fundamental justifications were scientific ones. This is precisely what he would want to deny in respect to religious knowledge, and one would have a hard time understanding how he could assert it of moral or aesthetic knowledge as well, one must view this statement as qualified substantially by the careful description that follows of what constitutes empirical evidence.
27. *Thinking About God*, p. 78.
28. *Paths in Spirituality*, p. 63.
29. *Humanity*, p. 64.
30. *Principles*, p. 223.
31. Ibid., pp. 239—240.
32.
33. Ibid., p. 240.
34. Ibid., p. 224.
35. Ibid., p. 225.
36. Ibid., pp. 223—224.
37. Ibid., p. 224.
38. Ibid., p. 224. My attack on Macquarrie stems from such statements and those which immediately follow.
39. Ibid., p. 225.
40. *Existentialism*, p. 101.
41. Ibid., p. 92.
42. *Thinking About God*, pp. 16—17.

The Problem of History

The problem that presents itself most acutely in the writings of John Macquarrie concerns how to integrate a concept of historical facts with the understanding of existence which composes the framework of his theology. For Macquarrie, the facts are important and cannot be reduced to existential "self-understanding". The events surrounding the Jesus of history changed the world, and we must continue to insist in Christian theology upon their objectivity. But the reduction of Christian theology to existential self-understanding seems to strike at the heart of this claim to objectivity. Thus, Macquarrie acknowledges the need for a theology which refers to these events as something other than "self-understanding".

The problem, however, is that, while Macquarrie acknowledges the need for this integration of objectivity into self-understanding, he never actually accomplishes this integration. In fact, he seems to withdraw from any responsibility for such a task on the grounds that literal statements of fact are "speculative" and that speculation obscures the *meaning* of the faith, which is best explicated in terms of existential analysis.

I do not think Macquarrie is wrong in his basic approach to theology, which relies heavily of existential philosophy (though, of course, he says clearly that Christian faith is a step beyond existential analysis). He is also correct in saying that objective historical events are the true ground of Christian faith. But I submit that his denigration of speculation represents a self-defeating attitude toward what he terms the "objective-historical". And, further, it lands him in the position which he criticises in Bultmann, even though he avoids following the whole-hearted project of demythologization that Bultmann pursues. He believes that if the Christian faith is based on objective historical facts, something that happened in the world quite apart from human knowledge and interpretation, then the same criteria that judge what happened in any historical event may be relied on to judge what happened in the events surrounding Jesus.

This assertion needs some clarification, but even on the surface it seems true. We ought not to withdraw from making assertions about historical facts merely because they are theologically important. If we are willing to conjecture what "must" have happened—and, in some cases, what *might* have been the case—in historical studies of World War II or the French revolution, then theological importance should not be a caveat that all such thinking in its own area is "speculative" in the sense of "unfounded". If objective-historical facts are the ground of Christian faith, no theology which intends to explicate that faith can avoid statements about the nature of these facts. We cannot rest easy with an understanding of what these facts *mean* unless we can suppose that they are true for reasons other than a blind, assertive faith. We must press on into an adventurous investigation of what happened and decide how to describe the important events while acknowledging the legitimate roles of metaphor, interpretation, and existential selfe-understanding with the phenomenological ontology this implies. To judge this investigation as improper because it is "speculative" is to fail to perceive the proper role of speculation in historical thought (as well as in the sciences) and so to fail to perform our total responsibility for truth in theology. This speculation—governed, indeed, by criteria which prevent it from being blind, radical, or impetuous—does play a proper role in history and in the sciences: it formulates fruitful hypotheses which state the facts we shall suppose to be true and which function as guides to future investigation and *praxis*. Theology demands that this aspect of the search for truth be integrated into the self-understanding of the faith which makes Macquarrie's theology so accessible.

The Problem of Historical Facts

We should note immediately that Macquarrie originally forswore any ambition to propose a philosophy of history. He placed questions of actual historical fact in the same category as that of the study of the natural world in so far as both present an *ambiguous* picture of the world and require interpretation. History and nature, e.g., can both be interpreted either with or without reference to a concept of divine beneficence.[1] Faith alone is willing to venture into a providential interpretation of nature and history.[2] In saying this, Macquarrie is arguing that the knowledge-claims of science and of history are not sufficient for grounding Christian faith. Faith always involves an interpretation of the facts. But, while this may be true, Macquarrie seems to place so much weight upon the importance of interpretation that the question of facts, of the content of statements about history, is reduced to playing a "noumenal" role: we can say *that* they occurred, but we cannot say what they are. Since all questions of factuality are reduced to questions of interpretation in such a stance, we can define Macquarrie's early position as a *critical* one. We must, then, inquire whether Macquarrie's subscription to the critical stance in relation to history changes in his later works.

Macquarrie's earlier rejection of an attempt to formulate a philosophy of history which would comprehend the historical fact of Christ gave way somewhat in later writings.[3] He says that the historical appearance of Jesus Christ, which ultimately fulfills the promise of God to Israel, *implies* an underlying philosophy of history according to which concrete historical happenings of significance throw light on the meaning of history as a whole.[4]

But did Macquarrie really change his point of view? I think not. For he continues to emphasize the role of interpretation to the extent of leaving little room for talk about the discovery of the facts. Where two interpretations conflict, e.g., Macquarrie is more inclined to attempt a resolution by means of a third, more adequate interpretation than by reopening research into the facts.

This inclination does not, however, formulate itself as a philosophy. It is, rather, an emphasis in the way Macquarrie employs the theory that he does state. He claims, in fact, that we must try to discover the facts in any research concerning history or science. But he understands a fact precisely *as* an interpretation, so that the distinction between facts and the interpretations that elicit and enrich their meanings is erased. Science and history become interpretive activities, and all attempts to step "outside" of correct hermeneutical principles in order to speak of a way of understanding the facts which is not grounded in a proper interpretive activity is called "speculation".

We may raise the issue concerning whether I am chasing a will o' wisp when I speak of the "facts" as distinct from interpretations. After all, isn't Macquarrie correct in asserting that interpretation provides the context for facts, such that facts become recognized as such only as part of a wider interpretation of their total situation?

Certainly, if I am pursuing the unattainable in the facts, I am doing so only on Macquarrie's own advice; for he himself distinguishes between facts and interpretations. And I think that he is correct in doing so but inconsistent in not developing a means of fruitfully maintaining this distinction in a way that benefits theology. Even if Macquarrie is correct in understanding facts as elements within an interpretive matrix, we can distinguish between interpretations which simply try to account for "known" facts and those which are in dynamic relationship with them. This latter type of interpretation gives the facts the power to modify or even destroy its view. It so commits itself to the facts that if claims to uncover (as an act of faith) that it does not shrink from using them as assumptions in speculative sorties aimed at uncovering new facts while enriching the interpretive matrix as a whole.

While we can acknowledge that Macquarrie wants to maintain some kind of fruitful relationship between facts and the interpretive matrix in which they arise, we must ask whether he is successful in doing so and, if not, why he fails. We can begin by noting how Macquarrie understands the fundamental nature of the gospel.

The gospel is not simply a "message" in scripture which can be "read off". It requires interpretation. And the way the gospel is read in any one era is subject to the entire intellectual, social, and historical milieu of the era.[5] *Something* is there, changing form with each interpretation. But it seems that this "something" functions like Kant's "thing-in-itself": it must be there, but we can know nothing about it in itself. The content of revelation is absorbed into an understanding based upon an hermeneutic grounded in existential phenomenology. It becomes much easier to speak about the gospel in terms of how it transforms the person than in objective-historical terms. And Macquarrie is ready to call "speculative" many of our efforts to grasp this objective-historical content.

The corrective to this one-sided emphasis upon interpretation is not, however, a scientific history which presupposes determinism as an explanatory principle. A scientific history could never confirm the claims of Christianity. For it views Christianity as one historical phenomenon among others, comprehensible in terms of factors immanent in history. Thus, incarnation, atonement, resurrection, etc., which are supposed to be understood outside of such a frame of reference, cannot be objects of a scientific history. They are relegated to myth.[6]

This is not to say, however, that a scientific approach to history can have *no* role in theology. On the contrary, a scientific-historical study of, e.g., the resurrection may lead us to accept the fact of its occurrence even though it remains "unexplained". This in itself may lead us eventually to abandon the hypothesis that all historical happenings are of the same order and can be explained scientifically.[7] But the main import of this approach toward history seems, for Macquarrie, to be that of giving the *right to believe* what is indicated as having *possibly* occurred, even though no explanation for its occurrence can be found. The proper role of a scientific history seems to lie in demonstrating that the faith-claims of Christianity *cannot be disproved*, even if they are rendered improbable. Faith is not based on the results of scientific historical research but merely receives permission to exercise itself in the light of the failure of scientific history to damage it fatally.[8] This sort of historical study, then, cannot and need not positively establish the "facts" upon which the Christian religion is based. But Macquarrie's attitude toward it indicates that he believes only science can establish facts; and that leaves us wondering what the difference between a fact and an interpretation would be *outside* of a scientific approach, as in an existential approach to religious faith.

But, apart from this negative role which a scientific history can play, what is the true object of historical reflection? Macquarrie says, "Historical reflection has for its subject matter human existence in the world".[9] Divine activity is discovered in *man's* historical existence;[10] it is discovered through phenomenological and existential investigation as the faith-object of the project of self-understanding.

Macquarrie sees the main task of history as outlining not the facts of history but rather the possibilities of human existence.[11] He says, "Historical reflection is concerned primarily with possibility".[12] "Possibility' here means that historical reflection is directed toward the understanding of possible ways people can decide to act, think, feel, etc.; in short, it aims at uncovering ways of existing. And this is particularly true in the case of the historical facts upon which Christian faith is based.[13]

Macquarrie, however, is careful to stop short of reducing historical study to an exercise in outlining human possibilities. Indeed, such an exercise would be impossible unless some attention were paid to historical facts themselves. In reference to theology this means that one must grasp the Jesus of history as well as the Christ of faith.[14] The relationship between knowledge of human possibilities and historical fact is perceived as a kind of circle: a preunderstanding of our existential reality is necessary in order to grasp anything of history at all, and a grasp of history enriches our self-understanding. This is the way we grasp the gospel as a whole, both in its objective historical content and in its revelation of possibilities for human existence. Understanding is constituted by this self-correcting and self-modifying body of knowledge.[15]

This hermeneutical circle prevents the imposition of any totalizing metaphysical schema on history. Thus, it promotes the decisional character of human history. We can, after all, only understand history from within history, as participants in it. So, as Christians, we must begin to understand the Christ even from within his historical context and not via metaphysical concepts which are a-historical:[16] "In historical reflection, the reflecting subject participates in a peculiar way in the object of his reflection".[17] I.e., historical events are not just "happenings", like chemical reactions. The historian is affected by them, has an existential relationship to them.[18] He understands them by getting "inside" them. The cross, eg., becomes significant to us when we *accept* it as having the present power to transform our lives, though this does not mean subjectivizing the gospel events into "inner" events that took place only "within" the disciples and takes place only within us.[19] Rather, Macquarrie has in mind an understanding born of an imaginative participation with the life of the agents of history.[20] The historian brings his understanding of existence to history but brings back to this understanding an awareness of new possibilities and dimensions gained through this participative encounter with the historical object.[21] Self-understanding is, then, developed through this circular encounter, mutually self-enriching, with history.

This circular method of developing both self-understanding and knowledge of the historical object is the closest Macquarrie comes to developing a philosophy of history which encounters the facts of history. The question we must raise, however, is whether he follows through with the program he seems to suggest here or lapses back into an identification of such a project as "speculation". We can follow Macquarrie's lead in acknowledging that bare facts, even if we could reach them, can have no religious significance. Facts are facts only in the context of the search that reveals them; and the religious search, the search for ultimate meanings, yields facts which already have their meaning by virtue of their reference to the religious quest. But these facts are meaningful and can be relied upon as a justifying ground for faith only in so far as they bear the marks of truth, if only a truth that is uncertain yet fruitful in the context of faith. But what role does "speculation", the willing venture into imaginative supposition concerning the objects of historical research, play in this mutually enriching circle? Macquarrie suggests in what we have seen thus far that an imaginative interplay, grounded in but transcending the evidence toward an end determined by the project of understanding motivated by faith, would deepen our self-understanding. But he seems to withdraw from the task of speculation when the understanding moves in the direction of the object. We can see this one-sidedness in a more careful analysis of what he terms the "existential-historical" and the "objective-historical".

Notes

1. John Macquarrie, *The Principles of Christian Theology,* revised ed. (London, 1977), pp. 240—241.
2. *Ibid.,* p. 241.
3. John Macquarrie, *Christian Hope* (Oxford, 1980), pp. 62—64.
4. *Ibid.,* pp. 62—64.
   Macquarrie suggests here that the radical reinterpretations of reality develop slowly in crises and sudden change. He indicates his reliance upon Thomas Kuhn's *The Structure of Scientific Revolutions.*
5. John Macquarrie, *Thinking About God* (London, 1975), pp. 52—55.
6. John macquarrie, *The Scope of Demythologizing: Bultmann and his Critics* (London, 1960), pp. 70—71.
7. *Ibid.,* p. 72.
8. *Ibid.,* p. 73.
9. *Ibid.,* p. 81.
10. *Ibid.,* p. 82.
11. John Macquarrie, *Studies in Christian Existentialism* (London, 1966), p. 166.
12. Macquarrie, *The Scope of Demythologizing,* p. 88.
13. *Ibid.,* pp. 88—89.
14. *Ibid.,* pp. 90—91.
15. *Ibid.,* pp. 87—88.
16. *Ibid.,* pp. 77—78.
17. *Ibid.,* p. 83.
18. *Ibid.,* p. 84.
19. *Ibid.,* p. 86.
20. Macquarrie seems to come close here to the position of Collingwood in *The Idea of History,* pp. 231—249.
21. Macquarrie, *Christian Existentialism,* p. 143.

The Existential-Historical and the Objective-Historical

In *Studies in Christian Existentialism* Macquarrie says, "An existential approach to Christianity does not deny that there are objective facts of past history at its origin, but it rightly sees that a bare objective fact of past history has in itself no religious significance".[1] In some works, however, he goes beyond claiming that such an existential approach does not deny objective facts; he says existential historical events *imply* objective-historical events.[2] He understands the "existential-historical" as that which is significant for my existence in that it sets before me a present possibility, i.e., an "authentic repeatable possibility".[3] But in order for history to outline repeatable possibilities, the events described must once have been actual.[4] Thus, while the "bare" fact must be given significance by faith, and this significance cannot be totally dependant upon historical research, *some* kind of historical reality must adequately ground our faith.[5]

We can summarize this in Macquarrie's own words:

> That is not to say, of course, that there is no value at all in the objective-historical understanding of the New Testament record. There could be saving events only if there has been certain objective events . . . the objective-historical does have a certain relevance to theology, as we shall see. The full understanding of the mighty acts as saving events is bound up with the understanding of them as objective events in the world, related to prior, contemporary, and subsequent events. Yet we begin with saving events which imply objective events—not with objective events which are transformed into saving events. It is not the objective-historical elements in the mighty acts that is of primary importance for theology.[6]

The objective-historical, then, is the foundation of the existential-historical, which in turn offers a possible way of existing that testifies to the objective-historical events while no longer relying on any particular objective-historical claim as the important factor in describing the transformative power of the existential import of faith. Macquarrie says that we both *cannot* and *need* not know the details or the actual content of the objective-historical facts that ground Christian faith.[7] Where the Jesus of history is concerned, we cannot have certainty but must rely on faith to fill in the picture.[8] And this faith is already alive in the *kerygma* and the scriptures it produces, which are our only source of knowledge about Christ.[9]

In other passages, however, Macquarrie indicates that the existential-historical should be equal in "weight" to the objective-historical. He means that the latter must be seen as fully supporting the weight of the former.[10] The development of existential self-understanding within Christian faith must be supported by our faith that objective events took place which give grounds for our self-understanding. But Macquarrie immediately moves to an emphasis upon the existential-historical in theology. He says, eg., that the positive element of stressing the existential-historical is that it properly emphasizes the significance of the cross as presenting a possibility for new life and releases its acceptance from the criteria of rigorous historical research.[11] Thus, the cross and the resurrection can be understood as *present* possibilities of forgiveness and new life from the existential-historical perspective.[12]

Since Macquarrie places such heavy emphasis on the existential or "faith-interpretation" approach to the history that undergirds Christian thought, we can easily wonder whether he leaves room at all in theology for "rigorous historical research". In view of his further denial that the scriptures impress themselves as factual upon the average person and that the facts of the Christian event cannot be known through an immediate or imaginative encounter or through a sense of his "immediate power",[13] we must wonder how we can reasonably pursue the possibility of a growing understanding, however imperfect or partial, concerning the events surrounding Jesus.

But Macquarrie explicitly rejects Bultmann's attempt to reduce Jesus to an existentialist teacher.[14] Jesus must have had some effect greater than that of a mere existential truth on his followers, who were brought to a crisis of decision about *him*. Thus, he understands that the historical facts about Jesus are important for an existential understanding of him.[15] We cannot remain content with a knowledge *that* Jesus existed (as does Bultmann), because the "that" is not separable from the "what" of Jesus.[16] We cannot be indifferent to historical questions. We must attend to the preservation of a "minimal core of factuality" without which our faith would not be possible. Faith cannot operate in a dream-world.[17]

In order, then, for the *kerygma* to act as a basis for a faith-commitment that changes one's whole life, Jesus life must have been seen as a manifestation of the life-possibilities that faith aims at. Christianity could not have begun as an idea, for ideas do not change lives in the way Christian faith has.[18] In saying this, Macquarrie indicates that the change which Christianity has effected in the lives of people is itself evidence of truth in its historical claims. The "minimum core of factuality" may be established with high probability on the basis alone of rational inference from the presence of the Christian community and its documents and traditions.[19] This "core" is the ground of our reasonable confidence and reveals that Christians are committed to a realistic possibility of existence.[20] He says, "I think that theology can get along quite well with this minimum of factuality, which it needs in order to assure itself that the way of life which it recommends is a possibility in 'real' life".[21]

But how far is Macquarrie willing to go in search of these facts that constitute the minimal "core" upon which Christian faith is built? Can Macquarrie go beyond a statement *that* this core should exist toward a delineation of what it is? An examination of his works shows that he tends toward being content merely with the acknowledgment that *something* happened and reveals that he sets barriers in front of the task of penetrating beyond existential analysis into the historical content of events.

Let us begin this examination by noting what Macquarrie says about miracles. He acknowledges that the question "Did this really happen?" may be legitimate, but it is questionable whether it can ever elicit the genuine meaning of the text. The question concerning facts is legitimate only in so far as a text intends to convey facts. But most texts of scripture intend to convey something more than facts:[22] miracles are not reported merely as factual events; they *intend* to convey a *meaning* which only such events, whatever they are, can convey.

We can appreciate Macquarrie's interest in the meaning of an event. Naturally we want to grasp the deeper meanings of such events, and these may not be accessible apart from existential analysis of the total miracle-situation. But it is clear not only that Macquarrie stops doing theology at this point but also that he expects that theology should not continue raising the historical question once the deeper meanings of the event become accessible through existential analysis.

Macquarrie seems to believe that Christians give their faith-commitment not to the facts of history but to the *kerygma*, the preached Christ. The preached Christ is the Christ whom God raised up and not merely the man who came to life again. And the most important events of Christ's life are understood in terms of a relationship to God which cannot be comprehended merely in terms of historical facts.[23] The Jesus of history and the event of Christ are not strictly identifiable. The Jesus of history can be seen as the "nucleus" of a total event that includes the *kerygma*.[24] And this nucleus can never be given an independant objective-historical status, nor can it be absorbed into the *kerygma*. But the meaning of the *total* event must be understood existentially, i.e., from the point of view of how he transforms human life and existence.[25]

According to Macquarrie, this way of seeing Christ is really no different from the way in which the disciples viewed him. They had no advantage over us.[26] They understood Christ more in terms of his meaning—his impact for transforming human life—than in terms of his objective-historical presence as a human being. The ministry and reality of Christ so affected his disciples that they saw the Old Testament radically anew, seeing Christ on every page regardless of the original intention of meaning. This was not a wrong interpretation, even when the facts were stretched to make Christ fit Old Testament prophecies. For this was not straightforward exegesis, which would see such distortions as wrong. Rather, these were interpretations which believed that a new depth of meaning was being discovered of which the original authors were unaware. These interpretations went beyond what was experienced in the historical-objective encounter with Jesus to a faith-interpretation of the "surplus meaning" in the messianic prophecies.[27]

This flowering of interpretive effort points to the genuinely creative power of the total event of Christ. But Macquarrie's emphasis upon theology's task as an existential analysis of this appropriation shows clearly that the Jesus of history, though a *sine qua non* of the Christ-event, is not to be viewed as the object of theology except as a "noumenal" reality about which we can say little. Macquarrie seems to end up in a position similar to that of Bultmann, who also adopts a critical stance in relation to historical issues.

Whether it is *necessary* that Macquarrie's position end up so much like that of Bultmann's is another question. Macquarrie believes that Bultmann himself never intended to cast such dark shadows on the adventure of enriching our knowledge of the historical facts that are so important theologically to a "whole" understanding of Christ. And he explicitly separates himself from Bultmann's own default on this point. But he himself never engages in the battle for historical enrichment; and he is not required to do this in order to make the theological points he has chosen to pursue. The reason why I state that his failure to so do is some kind of fault is that his reasons for choosing not to pursue historical knowledge are too potent for his purposes. He would be justified in simply addressing other theological issues; but he justifies addressing them by claiming that there is an *a priori* limit to the historical enterprise which has essentially been reached and which mitigates the usefulness of further research when more important existential analysis remains to be done. He decries "speculation".

But I believe there is room for Macquarrie, in an adventurous mood, to admit that intellectual exploration, imaginative hypothesizing, and a living faith commitment can work together to create a deeper, richer, more adequate overview in which human and divine truths are integrated into new conceptions. In a word, there seems to be room in Macquarrie's theology for the speculation which, because of an existential bias in his thinking, he prefers to avoid. And such speculation[28] seems to be the key to the achievement of new conceptions which rely on a cycle of factual enrichment and existential deepening.

Notes

1. John Macquarrie, *Studies in Christian Existentialism* (London, 1966), p. 111.
2. John Macquarrie, *An Existentialist Theology: A Comparison of Heidegger and Bultmann* (London, 1955), p. 171.
3. Loc. Cit.
   One suspects the influence of Kierkegaard and Heidegger in this characterization of an "existential-historical" object of knowledge.
4. *Ibid.*, p. 178.
5. John Macquarrie, *The Scope of Demythologizing: Bultmann and his Critics* (London, 1960), pp. 92—93.
6. Macquarrie, *Existentialist Theology*, pp. 170—171.
7. Macquarrie, *The Scope of Demythologizing*, pp 96—97.
8. *Ibid.*, p. 247.
9. Macquarrie, *Christian Existentialism*, p. 140.
10. Macquarrie, *An Existentialist Theology*, p. 280.
11. John Macquarrie, *Principles of Christian Theology* (London, 1977), p. 179.
12. Macquarrie, *An Existentialist Theology*, p. 172.
13. Macquarrie, *The Scope of Demythologizing*, p. 247.
14. Cf., Appendix A.
15. Macquarrie, *An Existentialist Theology*, p. 23.
16. John Macquarrie, *Thinking About God* (London, 1975), p. 209.
17. John Macquarrie, *God-Talk* (London, 1967), pp. 234—235.
18. Macquarrie, *Studies in Christian Existentialism*, pp. 148—150.
19. Macquarrie, *The Scope of Demythologizing*, p. 245 and *Christian Existentialism*, pp. 148—1250.
20. Macquarrie, *Christian Existentialism*, pp. 148—150.
21. Macquarrie, *The Scope of Demythologizing*, p. 99.
22. *Ibid.*, p. 39.
23. Macquarrie, *Christian Existentialism*, p. 142.
24. Macquarrie, *Thinking About God*, p. 22.
25. Macquarrie, *The Scope of Demythologizing*, pp. 178—179.
26. We can see the influence of Kierkegaard in this claim. Cf., Soren Kierdegaard, *Philosophical Fragments*, rev. ed., trans. by Howard Hong, Princeton, N.J.: Princeton U. Press, 1971, pp. 68—88.
27. John Macquarrie, *Christian Hope* (Oxford, 1980), pp. 65—67.

Interpretation

Macquarrie clearly wishes to avoid the excesses of Bultmann's program of demythologization.[1] But this does not mean that he will reject all efforts to apply hermeneutic techniques to history and scripture. On the contrary, he affirms that *interpretation* is required when we no longer share the presuppositions of a shared community of discourse, such as those found in scripture. And this is certainly true in the case of myth.[2] Theology attempts to interpret the Christ who meets us only in tradition by means of categories of our own time which are continuous with that tradition.[3] Macquarrie will, then, rely on what he calls "interpretation" to perform the translation of meaning from its context in an ancient community (and here the technique of demythologization will have a limited validity) to a frame of reference which is shared or common to us. Interpretation will "uncover" the meanings that are "hidden".[4] Interpretation, or hermeneutics, moves from the known to the unknown and back again to the known. It explicitates, corrects, and enlargens the known as it returns to it. It moves between two modes of expression (in theology, specifically, it moves between the symbolic language of revelation and existential-ontological language) and always points to fuller meanings behind paradoxes.[5]

Clearly, many of the stories of the Bible are indeed myth. Macquarrie seems to understand Biblical myth as true, however, in the sense that myths embody religious truths which can be made explicit through a correct kind of interpretation, an interpretation grounded in existential thought.[6] This thought is not an application of a system of ideas to a context to be interpreted but is more like an attitude or commitment to understand by relating the ideas found within myth or scripture to the common understandings found generally in human existence.

Existential interpretation, the key methodology which Macquarrie proposes is, however, a "rational" procedure.[7] It includes both scientific analysis and logical analysis of the text. Scientific analysis is necessary for determining what the text *is*, in so far as this is possible within a procedure that itself involves human creativity and artfulness, which all keen scientific analysis involves.[8] And logical analysis is not only necessary for a scientific analysis of myth but also in constructing a theory about myth in general, which requires consistent theoretical thought.[9] Thus, interpretation aims at grasping the

59

meaning of a text and conveying it *intelligibly* to the modern community seeking an understanding of it. It mediates intelligibility.[10]

The process of interpretations begins with an assessment of the measure of "sympathy" or affinity of interest between the interpreter and both the subject matter and culture which produces it. There must be some common areas of understanding which act as a "base" for interpretation.[11] Some of these areas may be only *tacitly* understood;[12] but, no matter how clearly or vaguely one comprehends a subject matter, this understanding acts as a guide to fuller, more explicit statements of meaning. Macquarrie would propose a hermeneutic that is at once both scientific and existential, which begins in a broadly based understanding of humanity and moves toward a more specific understanding of texts produced in former times by different cultures. In this way, the specifically less familiar becomes more comprehensible as we develop the more general, human meanings of the texts.[13]

Macquarrie calls the tacit understanding we have of a text, which is grounded ultimately in our sympathetic, human connection with all human artifacts, a "pre-understanding". The pre-understanding that we bring to the subject matter allows us to penetrate somewhat into its meaning; it is a "stage" for the hermeneutical advance. But this stage itself is a growing, vital tool in the hermeneutical task. As the meaning of a text grows clearer under an effort guided by a tacit understanding of its whole milieu, the explicitated meaning reacts on the tacit understanding so as to enlarge, modify, or correct it.[14] The hermeneutical task is "circular" in the sense that the proper development of one side of the interpretive process developmental yields material for the other side.

This circular movement is understood to be a circular interrelation of description and interpretation. Every description tends to become an interpretation, and all interpretations claim reference to "solid" descriptions.[15] The word "description" here signifies what Macquarrie means by "fact". Interpretation relies on facts, and facts support interpretations.[16] Macquarrie extends this relation not only to the fact-interpretation cycle of Biblical hermeneutics, but also to the manner in which the results of Biblical hermeneutics are relied upon for the wider interpretive work of systematic theology.[17] Human knowledge in general seems to advance *via* the hermeneutic circle of the mutual development of fact and interpretation.

The "common ground" or "shared pre-understanding" which acts as a stage for an investigation into scripture is human existence itself,[18] in addition to a few accidental characteristics we might share with scriptural authors. For Macquarrie, there is no radical disjunction between God and man. God is approached through an understanding of man, and man is comprehended only in the context of a developing idea of God.[19] We must develop both sides at once and by means of each other.

We can sum up Macquarrie's concept of the fact-interpretation circle by noting how it works where it is most explicitly used in theology: in Biblical interpretation. First, the exegete must be open to the Bible as a whole, even though he must also select the material that is relevant to his study. He must recognize that the Bible says many different things in different places and that not all statements are of equal value. His selection of "relevant" material is not, however, arbitrary nor made solely in support of a pre-conceived theory. It aims at giving the most *adequate* interpretation of the authentic message of the Bible.[20] This interpretation must aim at disclosing:
1) the author's intention[21]
2) the author's consistency and clarity
3) the modes of writing within one work (fact, reflection, command, etc.)
4) unconscious meanings.

And in disclosing these elements of meaning, the interpreter is responsible not just to the text or to the presuppositions of modern culture but to both sides at once. We must explicate the text responsibly by moving in a circular movement between the "facts" of history, philology, etc., and the total fabric of our self-understanding, including, of course, the cultural life in which it has evolved. This total understanding is a grasp of the *meaning* of the text. The achievement of this kind of understanding in theology is our true task in this field; it remains our prime theological responsibility.[22] And we fulfill our responsibility to the text when we seek the same thing the author intended to convey; i.e., when our *interest*, in the context of our own culture, corresponds to his and becomes disclosive of reality in similar ways.[23]

Our interpretive task, then, is a task which includes the entire venture of human knowledge. Interpretation moves between the effort to establish particular facts (with all of the scientific tools that requires) and the effort to connect the facts together into a creative synthesis. It conveys the meaning of the facts in such a way that our self-understanding modifies and is modified by our perception of the facts.

Meaning is *discovered* during this process because both interpreter and author share a common human existence which language never fully grasps but somehow always *signifies* beyond the situation of the author. When we enter into the language of the text to be interpreted, we contact not only the intended meaning of the author but also his "unconscious" intentions, meanings which are inherent in his language and his total existential situation and which contribute to the deeper, hidden significances of his intended meaning. Macquarrie, relying here on Heidegger, says,

> . . . interpretation can never be a manipulation, for the word has a life of its own, and the task of the teacher as preacher is to let it be heard. Words are not just dead things. They belong in the existential context of interpersonal communication, and, indeed, more than this, they belong in the very context of being. As Heidegger is

fond of saying, the word in the 'dwelling-place of Being' . . . The word has kind of a life of its own, so that even when someone says something, he may well be saying more than he consciously intends . . . (yielding) almost inexhaustible interpretations. Yet such interpretation has to be guarded and limited by the text and by a sound hermeneutical science.[24]

We can conclude this section on Macquarrie's notion of interpretation by noting that his approach to Biblical hermeneutics is quite different from that of Bultmann's program of demythologization.[25] The latter is more narrow in scope than existential interpretation. Further, it does not involve the understanding of ethical precepts in scripture, and it does not always manage to bring one to a vision of new practical possibilities for living. At best, it offers only a general, existential comprehension which remains sceptical concerning objective events, even where it need not be. Macquarrie, on the contrary, has developed a comprehensive mode of interpretation which includes both self-understanding (existential interpretation) and a comprehension of the facts.[26]

But we must note also that Macquarrie does not tell us what these facts are. He tells us that they are essential to the theological enterprise and gives us a methodology whereby we might think we can justify our factual claims. But when it comes to the crucial facts, Macquarrie does not follow through with a justified polemic. He falls back on stressing the *existential* meaning of the fact while relegating the actual historical event (the "objective-historical") to the "noumenal" status of being necessary for existence of phenomena which are supposed to be contingent upon it while not being comprehensible in themselves. And, while mystery may well be a necessary element of the event, Macquarrie prevents any serious attempt to discern what may discernible as facts by denigrating such attempts as "speculation". We can examine, as examples of this attitude, what Macquarrie says about the nature of Christ and the most important event concerning him, the resurrection.

Notes

1. Cf., Appendix B.
2. John Macquarrie, *God-Talk* (London, 1967), p. 75.
3. John Macquarrie, *Principles of Christian Theology* (London, 1977), p. 307.
4. *Op. Cit.*, p. 75.
5. Macquarrie, *Principles of Christian Theology*, pp. 37—38.
6. John Macquarrie, *Studies in Christian Existentialism* (London, 1966), pp. 103—105.
7. Macquarrie, *Principles of Christian Theology*, p. 243.
8. Macquarrie, *God-Talk*, p. 152.
9. John Macquarrie, *The Scope of Demythologizing: Bultmann and his Critics* (London, 1960), p. 199.
10. *Ibid.*, p. 35.

11. Macquarrie, *God-Talk*, p. 151 and *The Scope of Demythologizing*, pp. 45—46.
12. Macquarrie, *God-Talk*, p. 149.
13. *Ibid.*, p. 150.
14. *Ibid.*, p. 149.
15. Macquarrie, *Principles*, p. 182.
16. *Ibid.*, p. 183.
17. *Ibid.*, p. 183.
18. Macquarrie, *The Scope of Demythologizing*, p. 47.
19. *Ibid.*, p. 43.
20. *Ibid.*, p. 170.
21. *Ibid.*, pp. 39—40.
22. *Ibid.*, pp. 37—38.
23. *Ibid.*, p. 41.
24. Macquarrie, *Principles*, pp. 456—457.
25. Cf., Appendices A & B.
26. Macquarrie, *The Scope of Demythologizing*, pp. 15—17.

The Resurrection

We can illustrate much of what we have said thus far about Macquarrie's concept of existential understanding and interpretation by analyzing the manner in which he handles the issue of the resurrection, a central theme of Christian theology. I have chosen the theme of the resurrection to illustrate Macquarrie's theological approach because it is at once the most widely interpreted as well as disputed purported event of the Christian tradition and the most important of all historical traditions of the faith. One would think that Macquarrie's emphasis upon a two-pronged approach via factual discovery and existential interpretation would enable him to come to definite conclusions about the factual reality of the resurrection as well as to offer an interpretation of this and related events in the Christian tradition. And his theology should be a source for deepening our total comprehension of God and man, opening new possibilities of life. But Macquarrie does not follow through with the implication of his own theological approach.

To begin with, we may note that Macquarrie is properly sceptical about "extreme" approaches to scripture. He is sceptical, e.g., about the contribution of a "scientific" philosophy of history to our understanding of the resurrection—or any question of factuality in the Christian tradition. Such an approach, if it reduces the concept of the fact to that of the "verifiable" (*via* the senses), gives us a tendency to exclude any notion of God acting in history. It excludes *a priori* what it should credit or discredit only *a posteriori*.

On the other hand, we have seen that a purely existential philosophy of history (as represented by Bultmann and Buri) reduces Biblical events to possibilities of human existence. Neither of these philosophies is capable of conveying the significance of such events as the resurrection. Some other philosophy of history is required.[1]

Macquarrie is not, however, willing to adopt what he considers to be the most popular alternative to the line of theological thinking that extends from Kierkegaard through Heidegger to Bultmann, i.e., the line of thought that extends from Hegel through Marx to Ernst Bloch. This approach emphasizes the imminent development of the human spirit within history and would assert that the resurrection is "real" in the sense of being a "non-paralleled" event which is inherently incomprehensible but which we will someday (in the future) understand.[2] Macquarrie points out that, while this approach preserves some notion of the historical reality of the resurrection, it makes that reality an "empty" concept, not to be understood until human life achieves a certain level of thought. And this is simply to say that we do not now know anything about the resurrection but are relying on the faith that it occurred and that we will someday understand it. The problem is that we deny in actuality the very knowledge which we hope we will later achieve. Thus, we actually make the resurrection a mere faith-claim.

In the light of this rejection of an "empty" faith-claim, we must be surprised to find Macquarrie making a similar empty faith claim. For he says on one hand that, in order for us to speak reasonably about the resurrection as an historical event grounding the Christian faith, the resurrection must have an objective-historical base (all of the historical witnesses indicate this, and the existential-historical meanings of the event of the cross necessitate its historical objectivity).[3] He asserts on the other hand, however, that there can be no "proof" of the resurrection and that faith could not in any case be grounded in such a proof.[4] And, while we may agree with Macquarrie on this point, we get a clearer view of his attitude in the following passage:

> We do not prove—or accept without proof—that something once happened, and go on to deduce what that happening now means for us. We begin with the present possibility which Christ offers in the proclaiming and hearing of the Word, and from that we infer that something did once happen, *but precisely what that something was is a matter for academic speculation only and of no particular relevance to faith.*[5]

This passage, more than indicating the status of faith in the resurrection in the context of historical investigation, displays a far more important *attitude* toward the relation between faith and whatever we may count as factual knowledge. Here, Macquarrie asserts that our faith *that* the resurrection occurred is to be maintained above any particular content which academic speculation might give to this faith. He supposes that, by doing this, faith becomes *immune* to factual objections. And this idea presupposes that faith can somehow function independently of "belief" in particular "facts". Thus, Macquarrie takes up the attitude that faith is primarily an attitude which is ready to ascribe some sort of reality to the crucial events of the Christian tradition without making *any* demand for conceptual content. "Academics" are, of course, free to speculate on the "real" nature of Christ and the event of the resurrection; but such speculation should have no effect on our faith, which functions independently of it. The "facts" which such speculation might propose should have no claim on Christian *faith*, which is the true subject of theology.

I believe that this attitude is an unfortunate barrier to the development of an essential element in the intellectual task of theology: the courage to risk the loss of faith in the face of disconfirming evidences which challenge it. This courage is implied in the word "faith", which indicates, at least partly, an attitude of belief not *fully* justified by what we otherwise claim to know. Faith involves a risk that one might be wrong, even when the whole person relies for life and sanity on it. This risk implies that we must remain conscious of disconfirming evidences and be ready to meet their challenge by an intellectual exercise which enters into factual dispute wherever the challenge warrants it. Faith is not, then, merely an "attitude" or "value" we take up in relation to the world. It includes an openness to all of the elements of life and thought which demand to be integrated into faith so as, altogether, to constitute the *content* of faith. And "speculation" is precisely that exercise or reason which ventures beyond, though not contrary to, the evidences in order to weld our whole world of beliefs, facts, emotions, values, and attitudes into a more integrated whole, reflecting the health which faith is supposed to purchase for us.

Macquarrie confirms that a reasonable faith must function without "proof" while avoiding contradictions or beliefs that are clearly contrary to the evidences. The sceptic, e.g., can always explain away the primary evidences of the gospels, such as the empty tomb and the appearances. But the faithful can, without irrationality, comprehend these as the supreme act of God's self-giving love.[6]

Such a faith is rational because it relies on evidences that are not discredited merely for being "explained away" in the context of a philosophy of history that *a priori* chooses to deny the possibility of an objective-historical fact such as the resurrection. One cannot, e.g., believe easily that the church grew on the basis of an hallucination of the resurrection. Such things occur in certain well-known circumstances in which a strong element of expectation plays a key role in inducing hallucination. But the resurrection was precisely a contradiction of all that was expected and hoped for.[7]

Further, the nature of the resurrection appearances themselves, combined with the profound significance of death and of sin and guilt (and release from these!) for human existence, provide a continuing testimony of the objective-historical content of the resurrection claims. In the first place, though the claim of a bodily resurrection is confused in the New Testament records, the claim of some sort of "bodily" appearance and of the empty tomb are consistent. But it is clear that the body of the risen Lord was different from the body as it is normally experienced and understood. This uniquely new kind of body was, however, continuous with its former one. And, Macquarrie says, this allows us to construct an analogy: Jesus is to the resurrected Christ (as conveyed in the experience of his followers) as the disciples' experience of the resurrected Christ is to our experience of a life dead to sin and revivified through Christ. The continuity inside transformation that occurs in our own faith-encounter with the risen Christ is symbolized in the objective-historical event of the bodily resurrection of Christ. But just what the content of this resurrection event is we cannot say without "speculation".[8]

Macquarrie emphasizes the Bultmannian line of thought, even if he pays a necessary homage to the objective-historical content of the resurrection. He says, "The basic idea of the resurrection is that life is stronger than death, that man never finds himself in a dead end but that always a new possibility opens up".[9] For him, a very important meaning of the resurrection is that it indicates the continuous possibility of the emergence of a new level of human and personal existence,[10] an emergence that is necessarily a part of this life. Our "resurrected" life begins in the moment of faith. The resurrection reveals that the God-centered life cannot be broken by death but gives new life to those who believe. It places the potential for emergence of novelty in the power of God.[11]

These general statements lead us to question not only whether Macquarrie can apply *substance* to what is thus far an empty intellectual commitment to assert that *something* happened on Easter Day but also whether any objective content *other* than that of a number of existential possibilities can be given to the eschatological expectation of the "general resurrection". Certainly Macquarrie believes, with Bultmann, that "death" (in the sense of the closure of human possibilities of existence, which may occur in life as well) is overcome in the God-centered life which arises in the face of an encounter with the risen Christ. But this "risen Christ" does not need to be understood in any other terms than those which faith in him creates out of the existential transformation which procedes from such faith. The understanding of the objective-historical content of the resurrection is relegated to speculation.

This ambiguity concerning the formal assertion but virtual denial of the objective historical content of the resurrection has its correspondence in Macquarrie's conception of the eschatological resurrection. Again, "some sort" of "after life" is indicated by the reality of death itself, which leaves our nature "unfinished" at its touch.[12] But Macquarrie does not follow the traditional view that the general resurrection is to be patterned after the resurrection of Jesus. One may legitimately suspect that the reason for this divergence lies in his refusal to give any objective-historical content to his concept of the resurrection of Jesus. In any case, he proposes that the eternal life corresponding to our eschatological expectation is connected to a kind of final "eternal now" of God, whose vision takes in at once all that we hold as past. Macquarrie says this is a final, consummating vision which allows us to live in some kind of intense communion with God (We are not "absorbed" into His own being). He denies that we will be "clothed with a spiritual body" as though it were a different kind of flesh,[13] but asserts instead that we are resurrected in the sense of being caught up in God's vision—remembered—as the psychomatic unities we are. In the context of this kind of existence, we outselves will heal the past and proceed toward a higher final consummation.[14]

I will not here enter into an analysis of Macquarrie's eschatology. By his own admission, he is adventuring into the realm of speculation and is applying keen insights into the subject of eschatology which are consonant with an existential ontology. Further, we will not raise the issue concerning the nature of our resurrected existence as part of the final "vision" of God. Macquarrie is not able and is not trying to give us any deeper view of these things at his present level of insight. But we can note that his inability to give objective-historical content to the "Bodily" resurrection of Jesus has the important consequences of making ambiguous the language in which we speak of our salvation and the nature of the God-centered life as well as of muddying our eschatological picture. Even Macquarrie's brief sally into speculation does not save him from the charge of ambiguity, though we must confess that no one can achieve ultimate clarity on such a question.

Notes

1. John Macquarrie, *Christian Hope* (Oxford, 1980), p. 102.
2. John Macquarrie, *Thinking About God* (London, 1975, pp. 225—229.
3. John Macquarrie, *Principles of Christian Theology*, rev. ed. (London, 1977), p. 187.
4. *Ibid.*, p. 188.
5. John Macquarrie, *An Existentialist Theology: A Comparison of Heidegger and Bultmann* (London, 1955), pp. 188—189 (underlining mine).
6. John Macquarrie, *Principles* (London, 1977), pp. 288—289.
7. John Macquarrie, *The Faitrh of the People of God: A Lay Theology*, p. 63.
8. Macquarrie, *Christian Hope*, pp. 67—80.
   Macquarrie, in *The Humility of God* (London, 1978), pp. 72—76, extends his concept of the "new body" of the resurrected Christ so far as to cast some doubt on whether he believes in a bodily resurrection of Christ in any normally meaningful sense of the word "bodily". His insistence that any theory about the actual event of the resurrection must remain speculative, combined with this development of an almost non-bodily "bodily" resurrection, can be taken either as his own daring sally into speculation (against which I am not opposed) or as a withdrawal from the claim of a bodily resurrection. Such a withdrawal, however, would make the resurrection a "noumenal" event and undermines any attempt to say anything "factual" about this all-important historical event. Because Macquarrie's clearest statements about the nature of the bodily resurrection tend to emphasize the *difference* between the body of the historical Jesus and that of the resurrected Christ, we must interpret his statements that the concept of the bodily resurrection must ultimately remain speculative *as a failure to pursue the objective-historical content of the event.* And the proclivity for this failure is entrenched by an *a priori* caveat against "speculation", which Macquarrie unwarrantedly indentifies with irrationality and unjustifiable departures from the evidences.

9. John Macquarrie, *The Concept of Peace* (London, 1973), p. 73.
10. Macquarrie, *Principles*, p. 305.
11. *Ibid.*, p. 289.
12. Macquarrie, *People of God*, p. 63.
13. This denial is entirely consonant with his difficulty in assigning any objective-historical content to Jesus' resurrection and with the ambiguities in which he involves himself conceiving it.
14. John Macquarrie, *In Search of Humanity: A Theological and Philosophical Approach* (New York, New York, 1983), pp. 251—252.

John Macquarrie's Phenomenological Ontology

Thus far we have examined Macquarrie's first level of truth. Now we turn to the second level of knowledge, which constitutes an ontology grounded in the phenomenological method. This method demonstrates that an understanding of Being develops out of higher reflection upon the experiences constituting the first degree of knowledge. These reflections are not just undisciplined insights but constitute an ordered and disciplined description of Being based on an existential-phenomenological analysis of human-being.

Macquarrie considers phenomenology to be the method appropriate to a descriptive analysis of that which is revealed in man's own self-disclosure as existing.[1] Here we are dealing not with explanations (the assignment of "causes", etc.) but with what shows itself originally in experience. The result is an ontology based upon an existential grasp of man's being.[2] Taking into account the affective states of man as well as the drive to cognition, phenomenology requires "willing" oneself into a sympathetic participation in the reality being described, a reality that is publicly accessible and can be described in a way that "fits" and illuminates experience.[3] In order to see what discloses itself as being, phenomenology attempts as far as possible to "bracket" presuppositions, prejudices, and accepted interpretations, including the entire apparatus of science with its causal explanations. It deals with phenomena as structures of experience rather than as mere "subjective ideas" or as "subjective realities".[4] But as the phenomena are described and analyzed, recurrent patterns and structures emerge which enable us to classify and develop typologies of experience.[5] Pure description leads into theoretical structures which reflect with ever increasing adequacy the *aletheia* of Being.[6]

To be successful, phenomenological description must illumine the interrelationship between ideas. It allows us to "see in depth", e.g., the entire configuration of an idea or set of ideas as they become visible. In religious experience, e.g., repentance, conversion, sin, peace of mind, joy, anxiety, sense of presence, etc., are seen in their interconnections. The "logic" that pertains to such ideas and which defines them as circumscribed within a "domain" of thought comes into view through the on-going process of description. Entire belief systems emerge, illumined in their interconnections. And, in this way, a total vision of life may emerge.[7] Thus, we cannot be satisfied with a disjunction between the axiological-existential aspect of such knowledge, calling this aspect, e.g., a form of religious knowledge, and its "factual" side. We ought not to identify the religious elements of a knowledge claim with its "poetical meaning", while setting aside its factual claims as another sort of meaning. These are rather two *functions*: the poetical functions set forth a way of life, and the factual functions shed light of the problem of Being as a whole.[8]

Macquarrie seems here to be trying to claim some form of objectivity for existential-ontological knowledge. Certainly, one must agree that this knowledge, if it is indeed implied by and constitutes the ground for the factual knowledge forming the first level of *aletheia*, can hardly be relegated to the realm of subjectivity. How could it be less true than the knowledge it is supposed to ground?

But we need to raise the issue at this point whether Macquarrie's seeming implication that ontological knowledge is somehow factual should be taken at face value. Certainly, religious knowledge contains factual elements, since it arises out of a world which is understood to a large degree in terms of historical, scientific, psychological, sociological, and politico-economic facts. But, while we want to count the existential-ontological knowledge that an existential phenomenology discloses as the structural ground of facts in any of these domains (and as inherently linked to them within the parameters of each domain) as objective and, hence, true, we must pursue clarity where Macquarrie seems to slip from his own insight toward a confused notion. Thus, we should refrain from calling these truths factual. If we did call them factual, then we would find it necessary to distinguish between the *kind* of facts they represent and the sorts of statements which we ordinarily take to be facts. Macquarrie himself, however, does not remain consistent to the notion that existential-ontological knowledge is factual;[9] so we can better interpret his unclear and seeming intention to view it as such at times as a way of misspeaking himself. We need not speak of the "facts" constituting existential-ontological knowledge, even if we can now more clearly refer to the "factual side" of such knowledge, referring, of course, precisely to the facts that are *transcended* as we move toward this second level of *aletheia*. Existential-ontological knowledge has a factual side because it is an *implication* of the facts, though the sort of implication which is best disclosed through the phenomenological method. The knowledge we gain in the phenomenological method constitutes the epistemological ground for unfolding the deeper meaning of the facts as they relate to human existence. And, as such, it manifests the wider objective ontological dimension in which the various kinds of beings described factually in the various domains of knowledge participate and, indeed, gain their being. Existential-ontological knowledge is objective, then, because it moves out of facts to their deeper ground, which is best described as knowledge of the structure of human existence, which cannot be adequately grasped without moving even further onward to the ontology that parallels existential knowledge. The third level of *aletheia* will be developed as the sort of thinking ("primordial thinking") which aims at grasping the ultimate ground of this ontology and brings us face to face with the symbolic language of Being, which we already touch on in the delineation of existential ontology.

An ontology is complete in Macquarrie's view, then, only when it includes both the most intimate existential insights and the most "objective" insights into Being:

> When one has asked all the questions that can be asked about this human existence of ours, one still has to go on to ask the questions about that wider being within which 'we live and move and have our being'.[10]

This "wider" being is the object of ontology (or metaphysics).

> By a metaphysical concept, I mean one the boundaries of which cannot be precisely determined, not because we lack information but because the concept itself turns out to have such depth and inexhaustibility that the more we explore it, the more we see that something further remains to be explored. The more we grasp it, the more we become aware that it extends beyond our grasp.[11]

Macquarrie's affirmation of the necessity of developing an ontology based on existential phenomenology is not a reaffirmation of older forms of metaphysics:

> On the one hand there is a cutting away of the larger pretensions of traditional metaphysics. Just because of man's finitude, facticity, and historicality, he can never have a final view of the whole. Yet the existentialist refuses to join the positivist. Some glimpse of reality, he claims, is granted to men, however fleeting and fragmentary this glimpse may be. But language too runs out, and only indirectly can anything be said about reality.[12]

This indirectness is, however, no barrier to ontology. If we cannot evade such ultimate ontological questions as the existence and nature of God, we should move at least in the direction of an existential ontology which avoids the older style of speculative metaphysics and which forms a modern counterpart to the old-fashioned and largely discredited natural theology.[13] The key to this "new" ontology lies, for Macquarrie, in his understanding of Being as the "transcendent" of human existence rather than as a substance of some kind. As we noted in the analysis of *aletheia*, we move from a weak, pre-reflective notion of Being to a highly unified, deeply manifestive notion of it and to Being-fulness in various stages. This process begins in an awareness of Being as transcendent of our own existence, an awareness which grows out of our coming up against our limits as existents. Macquarrie follows Jaspers in describing such circumstances as "limit situations". At such times we can become open to Being, or experience something of the transcendence of Being, though we are always free, of course, to level everything down to the familiar and the manageable. To confront Being as transcendence is to confront it in a space which Jaspers calls the "comprehensive".[14] The "comprehensive" lies beyond the distinction between subject and object and is the source of insight into the ontological ground of the facts of ordinary life and of action grounded in such insight.[15] Existential-ontological knowledge does not come automatically, even if we possess what Macquarrie calls a "drive to know", which is part of the natural process of our drive to be, to fulfill the potential of human existence by discovering and entering into the fullness of Being. It requires *choice*, an existential act which deliberately seeks to relate us to Being in such a way that, by virtue of a more profound participation in it, our grasp of it deepens.

There is no clear demarcation between the second and third levels of *aletheia*, just as there is none between the first and second levels. But we can characterize all three according to their unique attributes. The prime attribute of the second level of knowledge is that it unfolds, as we choose to pursue it, the existential meaning of the factual realities of everyday life and manifests the ontological ground not only of these but of new and higher possibilities of existence and knowledge which are resident in the higher unities of Being.

How does Being begin to manifest itself as we pursue the ontological ground of the existential structures which phenomenology discloses? Macquarrie notes that there is an intimate relationship between what he, with other existentialists, identifies as Being and what is called "nothing". This relationship arises very naturally. Being, as a transcendent reality, is a generally forgotten dimension of our human reality; but we are still often "brought up short" by the need to recognize that this or that specific entity *is* or *is not* or is not as it *should be*. Macquarrie says that this noticing involves a noticing of Being; but it involves a noticing of nothing as well, since nothing is precisely what is noticed whenever we are struck by the *being* of an entity. For "nothing" is added to entities when we notice *that* they are. Macquarrie goes so far as to say that Being and nothing are the same.[16]

"Nothing" is not to be understood as a purely general idea of negativity. The logical notion of negativity in fact presupposes the nullity that belongs to existence itself. Clearly, the logic, or "language-game", by which nothing can be understood is different from that of traditional logic.[17] And, certainly, everyday object-language is not sufficient for this purpose. We need a different language and a different grammar, one based on a science of language which has a foundation that is ontologically more primordial.[18] It is this language which Heidegger tried to develop in *Being and Time*.

Macquarrie summarizes and adapts the results of Heidegger's earlier inquiry into nothingness by asserting four important meanings for the word "nothing":[19]

1) Nothing is the nullity we find in our own existence, our anxiety which discloses the possibility of ceasing to be.

2) It is what the everyday world becomes for us when we undergo the

transvaluation of values in the face of the end.

3) Nothing is a foil for Being in that it makes it possible for us to recognize entities as entities and awaken to the wonder of Being.

4) "Nothing" is identifiable with Being in so far as both Being and nothing are not entities, and entities are all that appear.

Macquarrie emphasizes the importance of the third and fourth meanings of "nothing". He agrees with Hegel that pure undifferentiated Being is the same as nothing. Only as entities does Being stand out from nothing. This nothing, however, is the ground of the primordial experience we have of Being: *wonder that there are beings and not just nothing*.[20]

It is at this point that Macquarrie, though a disciple of Heidegger, departs from Heidegger's form of existentialism. In *Being and Time*,[21] Heidegger characterizes *anxiety* as the basic mood through which we encounter Being. But Macquarrie, relying on a more positive interpretation of the nature of wonder, suggests that joy[22] is an ontological affect and is a better clue to Being. Joy may be a priviledged form of participation in Being whereby a more profound disclosure is given to us than that afforded by anxiety. Heidegger himself has intimated that this may be the case,[23] though it is Macquarrie who suggests that joy should be considered the prime disclosure of Being.[24]

Whether understood through the affect of joy or anxiety, however, Being is grasped as a "difference" from objects in our world, from beings. Hence, Macquarrie, along with most existentialists, distinguishes between being as such and factual beings. *Ontological* statements refer to the Being of something and to its possibilities of being, whereas *ontical* statements refer to an entity and to its relationship with other entities. Science, the first level of knowledge, is grounded in ontical knowledge. Every ontical statement, however implies an *ontological* one, since the former indicates only the realization of a particular *possibility* on the part of a being. Thus, the ontical can be clarified ontologically, i.e., a particular fact of being can be shown to fall within the scope of various possible ways in which an entity might *be*.[25] We understand the Being of an entity in terms of its possibilities rather than in terms of its particular concrete manifestation, though such an understanding can be gained only by letting Being disclose itself through and in terms of such entities and their particular factual states.

We must pause in this explication of Macquarrie's ontology to note that, to a large degree, this dissertation is concerned with the problem of the relationship between the factual ("ontical") status and the ontological status of knowledge. Macquarrie agrees here with Heidegger that the ontical is a particular fact which is essentially accidental. It implies the ontological structure which is the ground for its possibility. But the implication is not mutual. The ontological structure does not imply any factual entity or occurrence. Thus, a phenomenological ontology, even if it lays bare the structure of being itself, cannot judge concerning either what is (science) or what was (history) the case in the actual world.[26]

The issue which rises before us here concerns a fundamental dynamic in the development of the various domains of knowledge. As ontological knowledge develops, the wider unities of Being emerge into view. These consist of phenomenological descriptions of essential types of beings which may manifest themselves in a variety of ways in the actual world. They are at once more general and more real than any particular manifestation. This notion, which has always been at the heart of the universal-particular problem throughout the history of philosophy, has been the cause of much discussion. I do not intend to try to resolve the problem here, as it is only relevant in this discussion to indicate that Macquarrie is embroiled in this issue and develops much of his concept of the hierarchical order of Being in the face of it. More pertinent here is the question concerning whether Macquarrie is able to link universals and particulars in a way which is useful for theology.

Certainly, Macquarrie has effected a very tight linkage between the wider unities of Being which Heidegger calls "ontologicals" and the ontic particulars they ground, viewed from the epistemological movement from particular to universal—or, from ontic fact to the wider dimensions of ontological reality. Facts of ordinary life make sense only when grounded in wider ontological structures which themselves must eventually be viewed as manifestations of a Being that can be grasped only indirectly through symbol. Facts *imply* their ontological ground in the sense of being *bound* ontologically to it, so that they can be seen as participating in it. And we must suppose that our ontological categories themselves bear the same relation to our most profound grasp of Being.

But when we view this relationship in reverse order, from above downward, or from the ontological ground to the ontic fact, the tightness of this linkage relaxes a great deal. For, whereas when we move from particular to universal the ontological unity is kept whole as a matter of phenomenological implications, the implicatory structure of the relationship is destroyed when moving from ontological ground to ontic fact. Replacing it is a relationship of *meaning*: the particular facts become viewed as *accidental* manifestations which have their meaning described in the fuller ontological dimension which they finitely and partially manifest. One cannot begin with the wider ontological ground and deduce, especially by phenomenological description, any particular ontic fact. One can say in general what sorts of ontic facts *might* arise in the actual world from within some wider ontological ground, but one cannot deduce any particular state of affairs. These states of affairs represent only *possible* manifestations of being, not necessary ones.

The relevance of this observation concerning Macquarrie's phenomenological ontology lies in his tendency to identify religious language with a Christian interpretation of existential-ontological knowledge and, even more so, of the symbols and indirect language constituting primordial thought. In so far as he does this (and we must say in passing that there is no necessary reason to do so), then the same "one-way" direction of implication that applies to these levels of thought applies also to religious thought. Assertions of knowledge in the religious domain cannot lead to the assertion of any facts. We shall see that, though Macquarrie wishes to assert as a Christian that certain facts are true, his philosophical and theological relationship to these facts is at best tenuous. The real truths which constitute the domain of knowledge he considers religious are the deeper insights into Being, understood in the context of Christian faith as God, afforded by the progressive uncovering of Being in human thought. We have seen what sort of difficulty his existential philosophy poses for him in interpreting the meaning of historical facts that are essential in Christian faith. For we have seen that unfolding the meaning of these facts does not involve asserting their reality.

Since the contingent world is not implied by the higher unities of Being, there can be no purely rational integration of all domains of knowledge. Indeed, at least for the domains of science and history, the ontological contingency of the world is responsible for the proliferation of knowledge into domains. The finite, contingent human knower is already equipped to experience life only from various more or less integrated sensual, emotional, and intellectual aspects. And the world itself is only a finitely realized portion of the possibilities which we can discover in higher unities of being. Thus, factual knowledge of all sorts, moral knowledge, aesthetic knowledge, religious knowledge, etc., represent natural domains of experience because of the ontological contingency and finiteness of both knower and known. And this fracturing of human experience, which is to some degree grounded in and productive of the fracturing of human existence itself, can result only in an epistemological world of irreducible domains which interplay with one another in ways which can support, confirm, deny, or contradict the claims they make on each other.

These points become clearer in the context of some further analysis of Macquarrie's concept of Being as it impinges upon the third level of *aletheia*. He says that Being should not be understood as something "else" which stands behind the appearances of entities in the world:

> Let us begin by recalling that if Being is a *transcendens*, it is also immanent in the beings and is nothing apart from them; that if it is distinguishable from appearing, it yet includes appearing, and is not some supposed 'thing-in-itself' behind the appearances. The word 'Being' does not stand for some allegedly intangible, invisible, unverifiable being that exists in addition to the beings that we know in everyday experience, but stands for Being that gives itself in and with and through particular beings.[27]

Being, then, gives itself only in its appearances. All phenomenological ontology must begin with appearances. Appearances, however, are not sure guides to the Being of an entity. They lie between being and nothing in the sense that, though they themselves *are*, they may not be what they purport to be. Yet, when we accept appearances as they are, we gain the possibility of achieving the presence and manifestation of being.[28] This requires the proper use of the phenomenological method and existential insight. But eventually Being is "mediated" through the appearances that announce it.

What is it in man that is the occasion for this uncovering of Being? We have noted that Macquarrie believes man has a drive to know which cannot rest content with the knowledge that enables him to survive in the pragmatic world of everyday life. I have already described how this drive manifests itself in the discovery of levels of knowledge, which are parallel to levels of ontological development in the knower. Human existence "goes out" of itself toward Being; and this means it reaches out toward becoming more being-*ful*. On this primordial level of human reality, there can be no sharp separation of being and knowing: Being is disclosed in man's process of coming to full realization of his potential to *be* and know himself as being, in raising himself to a height from which he can see what discloses itself as Being. We do not "constitute" this higher disclosure as though it were an object of a science of which we are the inventor; Being reveals itself when we are ready to grasp it. It does not become visible only in terms of a light we are able to shine on it; it provides its own light by which it is known.[29] Being "emerges" in this way from what is hidden. Indeed, the word "nature" is only a bad translation of the Greek word *physis*, which is derived from *phuein* (transliteration mine), meaning the process of arising or emerging from the hidden.[30]

This arising or emerging is a process which corresponds to man's own ontological process of *becoming*. Becoming is the process which differentiates beings as particular entities from both Being and nothing. Becoming lies between Being and nothing, which are indistinguishable without the differentiation of "coming to stand out" in the guise of particular beings. The intelligibility we find in the world implies that the process tends toward order and not chaos or some kind of static being. Becoming moves toward some kind of unity and stability.[31] Being, then, is encountered in dynamic, active terms as a part of the vital world in which we live our everyday life; but its Being-fulness becomes more deeply known as we ourselves are ordered and stabilized by what we discover of it through our drive to know it.

Macquarrie, in his *Principles of Christian Theology*, gives us a characterization of Being based upon an existential phenomenology. First, we can understand what Being is not:

1) Being is not *a* being, something among things that are. We cannot say "Being is".[32]

2) Being is not the "absolute" in either the sense of a totality or as a sum of beings. This would make its being other than the sum and would require explanation in itself.[33]

3) Being is not a substance in the sense of a "substratum" underlying the phenomenal characteristics of beings. Substance is a static notion with thinghood as its model. Because of its tendency toward a kind of reification, a characterization of Being as the "ground of being" (Tillich) is to be avoided.[34]

4) Being is not a class, a single genus of things. For Being cannot be a property which pertains to things, so it cannot form a class which all things have in common. That Being is not a property is evident from the fact that nothing is added to the conception of a thing when we add "being" to its list of properties.[35]

We can see that these four statements about what Being is not are firmly grounded in the existential phenomenology that we have outlined. Being must be understood in terms of what appears without a presupposition of a being behind being. This makes assertions 2) through 4) necessary. Yet our own transcendence is the ground for understanding the transcendence of Being from beings and for perceiving the ontological difference between Being and beings.

These considerations enable us already to point to a characterization of Being from the third level of *aletheia*. Moving toward a more positive characterization of Being, we can note that the temporality of our own existence seems to contrast with another experience which we regard as somehow the inherent stability of Being. Being is the source of our own stability and unity in the face of the temporal changes that are inherent in our existence, and we experience Being as transcending our temporality. This does not mean that Being is eternal in the sense of "timelessness" or "unending duration". But it does mean that Being contrasts with our changeableness in its negative sense: the sort of changeableness which frustrates wholeness and destroys human unity and community.[36] Certainly Being is also temporal in that it is manifest in beings. They themselves are temporal and provide the only clues to Being, though they point beyond themselves in doing so, suggesting that Being is other than what they are.[37] Being, as eventually revealed in the third level of *aletheia* known as primordial thinking, is not a particular being in space and time. But it is more "beingful" than that sort of being, since beings *are* only by participation in Being. This "plus" of beingfulness does not refer to some sort of Platonic timeless realm or to a static world but to something which dynamically answers to the dynamic outreach of our existence in its totality as a willing, thinking, feeling, understanding being. It needs as its object something capable of like response. The matrix for understanding Being is our total existential situation. Thus, the method for achieving an understanding is a phenomenology based on an analysis of human existence which moves toward ontology. Being, then, gets characterized positively as that which encounters us in our total existential situation:

> Being, then, gets disclosed in existing. But existing is not just beholding or contemplating or perceiving, for it is also concern and involvement and participation. Feeling is always a constituent factor in existing. At any given time, feeling, understanding, and willing . . . are all there together in existing . . . and being is disclosed in affection and volition as well as in cognition.[38]

Again, "What is it then that confronts us and reveals itself when we have become aware of the nothingness of ourselves and our world? The answer is: Being".[39]

Why is it that becoming aware of "nothing" provides the key to the disclosure of being? The answer lies in the fact that being is experienced and defined as that which "overcomes" nothing. We touch the "back" of Being in an awareness of nothing. And Being is then experienced as a movement toward realizing the potentialities of being, as an answer to our hopes:

> . . . Being overcomes the nothing into which it has gone in creation; . . . although creation implies risk, nevertheless the movement is toward realization of potentialities-of-being, and the overcoming of dissolution, frustration, annihilation.[40]

These "potentialities of being" are not to be conceived in terms of the "things" of the world, such as material objects. In an existential-ontological view, the world is not substance but a structure of meaning. A thing is what it is in virtue of its place in an *intelligible* world. Its "objectivity" is bound up with its intelligibility, its having a meaning defined by a structure of intelligibility in which each part is related to another as part of the context of its meaning, its "sense". This represents yet another slant on the way Macquarrie resolves the problem of whether the world is "subjective" or "objective", since the question of "inner" and "outer" does not arise on the level of the original presentation of phenomena in experience.[41]

Sidestepping the question of the objectivity of Being by defining Being in terms of its original experiential presentation does not, however, allow Macquarrie to escape from the responsibility to say something about the ontological nature of this presentation. For, no matter whether we decide that this presentation is "subjective" or "objective", it *is* present as a primordial experience of Being; and this experience points to something beyond itself, since it grasps itself as a kind of "in-flowing", as something that has been released out of what is beyond itself. Macquarrie, along with Heidegger, characterizes Being as a "letting-be":

> . . . Being is the *transcendens*, it is already thought with every being, it is the condition that there may be any beings whatsoever. A being is a being in virtue of the fact that it is, but Being is not something that is prior to any is-ness. So while Being may be inseparable from beings, it is nevertheless dependant on Being, which lets them be. This letting-be is the creativity of Being, and the dependance of the beings is their creatureliness.[42]

> The expression which I prefer to use, however, to point to the characteristic of being as the condition that there may be any particular beings, is 'letting be'. Being, strictly speaking, 'is' not; but being 'lets-be', and since letting-be is prior to particular instances of being, though other than these, we are justified in claiming that being is more beingful than any particular being that it lets-be, and we have justification too for using, with proper care and qualification, the expression 'being is'.[43]

Macquarrie does not leave it to us to relate such a concept of Being to its obvious religious implications. He says, "The religious man experiences the letting-be of being as being's self-giving, the grace of being which pours itself out and confers being".[44] Thus, the primordial experience of Being's self manifestation can be characterized in such a way as to correspond to a concept of grace through the creative conferring of Being. The secular concept of Being as attained through a phenomenological ontology has profound resonances with the religious question.

But how are we to understand the dynamic of "letting-be"? A metaphor such as "releasing" or "letting" already implies a kind of activity. We have seen already how Being emerges into conceptuality through experience and reflection. And now we can understand how this emergence occurs not only epistemologically but ontologically as well. Indeed, the ground for the possibility that Being can emerge into conceptuality through understanding is that the Being in which we participate as human beings be characterized fundamentally as emergent. Thus Macquarrie can say that the emergence of beings is to be understood in terms of primordial Being's going out through expressive Being into the risk of creation.[45] Expressive Being is the dynamic, active outpouring or letting-be of Being; and Macquarrie uses the word "creation" in conjunction with such activity.

Resonating with Heidegger's question, "Why is there Being rather than nothing?", Macquarrie finds within the act of creative emergence itself an important clue which suggests an answer to this question. Beings seem to advance toward a fulfillment of a fuller potential characterized by a richer and more fully diversified unity. Further, each new stage in the progressive unity is more valuable than the one just before it. The creative emergence of Being in the context of beings seems to have some purpose rather than evidencing a pointless return to an undifferentiated unity of Being. Individual existents seem to be preserved to produce a higher existence. We can understand this more personally in the case of persons, who can form through acts of love bonds of unity which create higher forms of free, responsible human life.[46]

Again, the Being we have characterized in this preliminary way is not a vacuous abstraction but is a plenum, a whole, which holds in an ultimate unity all of its attributes. Macquarrie relates the wholeness of Being to the Old English sense of the word "holy". Being is holy in so far as it is whole.[47] But this implication of holiness in wholeness is not the sole reason for imputing holiness to Being. Macquarrie agrees with Rudolph Otto[48] that being is experienced as holy. It is mysterious and appears demanding, judging, overpowering (the "*tremendum*") as well as granting, saving, empowering (the "*fascinans*"). These ways of appearing, of course, correspond to the religious search and are not necessarily grasped in a purely secular consciousness. But the fundamental experience of a mysterious wholeness in Being which calls us to a deeper wholeness is part of every experience of Being. Such an experience is at the root of our understanding of God as righteous and just, stable and holy, graceful, loving, and merciful. But these are categories of faith rather than of direct experience, according to Macquarrie.[49] Nonetheless, we can now see more clearly how Macquarrie tends to identify the language of faith with a Christian interpretation of his ultimate language about Being.

Summary

In this section I have described the methodology with which Macquarrie pursues insight into the very nature of Being in order to show how he arrives at the more detailed conception of Being. This method is a descriptive analysis of human experience which brackets away the conceptual presuppositions that interfere with a grasp of the phenomena as they present themselves in our awareness. Because this analysis attempts to get at the original phenomena that underlie our conceptions of things, this methodology is called phenomenology. Macquarrie asserts that following the phenomenological method will allow us to see the "logic" and interconnections of ideas that present themselves in an enquiry, even to the point of the emergence of a total vision of life.

Phenomenology it not in itself, however, sufficient for satisfying our desire to grasp the deeper meanings of the phenomena that present themselves in human experience. The phenomena bear with them a reference to something beyond themselves, something that is not presented in itself. We cannot remain satisfied with the "hypothetical" structures of meaning which phenomenology alone gives, but must push forward, as a matter of the development of our own potential, toward an understanding of Being. Such an understanding is called ontology, and an ontology that is grounded in phenomenology is a phenomenological ontology. An ontology that is grounded in phenomenology is not a traditional metaphysics because it does not make many of the important distinctions that traditional metaphysics makes: the "subjective"-"objective" distinction, the substance-"spirit" dichotomy, and the fact-value dichotomy. Furthermore, instead of aiming at speculative knowledge, it relies on pointing indirectly at Being while claiming that indirectness is not a barrier to knowledge.

Indirectness is not a barrier to knowledge because the phenomenology Macquarrie proposes is itself grounded in an existential philosophy of man, where Being is always grasped as implicit and never fully recoverable in language. A grasp of our own journey toward the potential of a fuller being is the model Macquarrie uses for understanding the emergence of our understanding of Being through the discipline of phenomenology. As we attain greater being-fullness, our understanding of Being, though never "absolute", becomes more explicit.

The need for indirectness in ontology is grounded in Macquarrie's concept of the relation of indiscernability between Being and nothingness, a relation of such intimacy that beings cannot appear at all except in so far as they are "surrounded" with a nothingness against which they stand out and become apparent. Beings, then, manifest Being, which is the transcendent source for individual beings while being nothing apart from them. Ordinary object language cannot describe either Being or nothing; but human experiences such as anxiety and joy point to a sense of despair or fulfilment in life which discloses Being in a non-conceptual way. Ontology aims at making Being more conceptually explicit, though this can never be fully accomplished; and other epistemological projects, such as science, pursue the factual realities of everyday language, the ontical realities.

The search for Being, then, is not merely a scientific pursuit guided by the discipline of phenomenology, but our movement toward a form of personal being that seems to respond to a call from beyond itself. Such experiences as joy point to a wholeness in Being which transcends our temporality, promising deeper human unity and community, an "overcoming" of the nothingness that lies at the root of our despair and anxiety. We want to be in the fullest way possible, and we find in the transcendence of Being a "letting-be" that answers to our search for Being. The understanding of Being as letting-be provides not only an understanding of the dynamic by which beings appear in the world in their interconnectedness (so that ontical knowledge about them is possible) but also of how we move dynamically from lower forms of being and knowledge about Being to higher forms in which unity and stability act to preserve a sense of the wholeness that Being points to in itself. Macquarrie wants to assert that, if we refrain from stagnation or outright despair, an existentially based phenomenological ontology leads to the very brink of religion, in which our understanding of Being provides a matrix for unfolding much of the meaning of categories of faith, such as those of creation, grace, and the holy. Indeed, such categories, understood apart from a distinct Christian content, suggest themselves as part of the understanding of Being.[50]

I have suggested that Macquarrie's phenomenological ontology, while it may effect a fruitful way of understanding Being in ways which Christian faith can appropriate, presents a problem for understanding the historical and scientific facts that seem to be essential for Christian faith (e.g., the resurrection, Christology, Creationism, etc.). While one can move easily from an understanding of the actual world to a grasp of the general types of beings which ground these realized possibilities, one cannot move rationally in the reverse direction to speak of historical and actual scientific facts from a grasp of these higher unities of beings. As Macquarrie tends to identify religious knowledge and language with the understanding, translated into terms of Christian faith, that we have of Being as we move intellectually from "below" to Being, his religious knowledge lacks a means of asserting facts. Thus, he relegates the "facts" upon which Christian faith is grounded to domains of knowledge which he separates from religious knowledge, understanding them as bearing *meaning* for the Christian faith but not as knowable from within the project of establishing religious knowledge itself, a project which he understands in terms of the discovery of higher unities of Being. The essential facts of the Christian faith end up not being an essential part of the knowledge-claims in Christian theology. I have indicated that we must find a way to re-absorb factual language back into the project of Christian theology in order to make sense of these knowledge-claims and re-endow theology with its evangelical task of preaching a gospel that claims, as Christians generally believe, that God has touched the world and effected real changes as well as created joyful potentials for human existence.

Notes

1. Macquarrie is committed to the kind of phenomenology exercised in the existentialist tradition. He does not follow the Husserlian school of phenomenology into its inevitable brush with idealism, but appropriates the Heideggerian technique of making phenomenology a description and analysis of human existence. Thus, he does not bracket existence as part of the phenomenological reduction but views the descriptive process involved in the epistemological drive of phenomenology itself as an existential participation in the Being it describes.
2. John Macquarrie, *An Existentialist Theology: A Comparison of Heidegger and Bultmann* (London, 1955), pp. 35—37. We shall see that this emphasis on human existence involves a sharp distinction between what Heidegger and Macquarrie call the ontological ground of beings and the "ontical" or factual reality that they have.

3. John Macquarrie, *In Search of Humanity: A Theological and Philosophical Approach* (New York, 1983), p. 218.
4. Macquarrie's own interpretation of what phenomenology is does not attempt to pay homage to the Husserlian school, nor does he feel himself bound to a strict Heideggerian interpretation, though he follows Heidegger's break from "essentialist" thinking and affirms a phenomenology which functions in an existential context.
5. *Humanity*, p. 217. These "types" are what I term "domains" in respect to the unique areas or regions of knowledge they encompass.
6. This is a point in question: is it pure description *alone* which achieves this? Or must we engage in some rational exercise and both factual and causal investigations in order to achieve higher levels of *aletheia*? I shall argue that Macquarrie's concept of description, while useful in itself, is given too big a job to do. The higher levels of *aletheia* emerge only when we broaden our thinking beyond description to a fuller range of rational exercises. Macquarrie himself is not entirely true to this narrower notion of phenomenological description and does not wish to be true to it.
7. *Humanity*, pp. 218—219.
8. John Macquarrie, *The Scope of Demythologizing: Bultmann and His Critics* (London, 1960), pp. 127—128.
9. Indeed, in what follows we shall see that he maintains a firm distinction between the sort of knowledge he calls factual and the sort he calls existential-ontological.
10. *Demythologizing*, p. 128.
11. John Macquarrie, *The Concept of Peace* (London, 1973), p. 63.
12. John Macquarrie, *Existentialism* (Middlesex, England, 1972), p. 248.
13. Ibid., p. 273.
14. Karl Jaspers, *The Perennial Scope of Philosophy* (London, 1950), p. 162.

    The remembrance of Being is the prime characteristic of man that makes him human. Macquarrie understands the *awareness* of being as an *openness* to Being wherein Being is disclosed. Man is open to Being not only in the understanding but also in the affections and the will. And in each of these areas we have an awareness of Being which is manifested often in terms of inner contradiction and conflict. This conflict is interpreted as evidence that man is unfinished and is struggling to give birth to something better, something that can be revealed only as Being discloses itself in the future: in short, man exists in the sense of *transcending* his situation in all aspects of his concrete being. Macquarrie tends to identify "spirit" with this notion of transcendence, giving it a slightly more active meaning: spiritually, man has the creative possibility of rising above lower levels of life.

    The notion of man as transcendent provides a non-substantial model for understanding human reality. Man is not a "thing" which acts and reacts by mechanical principles but is, rather, characterized in terms of temporality. Existence is defined in terms of temporality. The self needs time to make itself. But this is not the time through which inanimate objects and animals perdure: moment to moment. Through memory and projection, two characteristics unique to man in the degree to which they are found in him, man can bring both past and future into the present, thus transcending the moment and constituting his identity throughout time. Macquarrie understands this act of projection to be an act of will which brings human beings into realization or actualization.

15. John Macquarrie, *Studies in Christian Existentialism* (London, 1966), pp. 80—81.
16. Ibid., p. 87.

17. Ibid., p. 84.
18. Ibid., p. 83.
19. Ibid., pp. 84—86.
20. *Demythologizing*, p. 87. Also, John Macquarrie, *Principles of Christian Theology* (London, 1977), p. 100.
21. Martin Heidegger, *Being and Time* (London, 1962), pp. 228—235.
22. To be fair to Heidegger, one must note that he was trying to disclose how *Dasein* in general becomes aware of Being. Few people are capable of finding the pathway of joy, though Heidegger would not discount it as a disclosive experience. He is not concerned to indicate the modes of disclosure which would be preferable over anxiety, perhaps because, even though his intent is descriptive, he himself does not believe that joy can be sustained as a disclosive experience. We might note in passing that Macquarrie, influenced by The Thomistic Tradition and the Aristotelianism that undergirds it, might have Aristotle's notion of the consciousness of the perfect celestial beings in mind: they contemplate the world in perfect joy.
23. Martin Heidegger, *An Introduction to Metaphysics* (Garden City, New York, 1961), p. 1.
24. *Existentialism*, pp. 171—172.
25. *Existentialist Theology*, pp. 30—31.
26. Edmund Husserl, *Ideas: General Introduction to Pure Phenomenology* (London, 1975), pp. 50—51.
27. *Principles*, p. 142.
28. Ibid., p. 112.
29. Ibid., p. 86.
30. Ibid., p. 223.
31. Ibid., p. 111.
32. Ibid., pp. 107—108.
33. Ibid., p. 110.
34. Ibid., p. 109.
35. Ibid., p. 108—109. Macquarrie is following Kant's Critique closely here (cf., *The Critique of Pure Reason*, B 268).
36. Ibid., p. 205.
37. Ibid., p. 142.
38. Ibid., pp. 97—98.
39. Ibid., p. 87.
40. Ibid., p. 243.
41. Ibid., p. 479.
42. Ibid., p. 211.
43. Ibid., p. 113.
44. Ibid., p. 114.
45. Ibid., p. 223.
46. Ibid., p. 360.
47. Ibid., p. 210.
48. Rudolph Otto, *The Idea of the Holy* (London, 1971).
49. *Principles*, p. 209.
50. Macquarrie's thought is so bound up with the categories of Christian faith that one must be careful to distinguish those concepts that are purely philosophical from those that are theological or dogmatic. This is not a particularly difficult task, since Macquarrie himself is careful to make this distinction as he unfolds his

Christian theology. Thus, even though his purely philosophical thinking is informed by Christian faith, he is quite clear about the scope of philosophy for theology. Philosophy leads us to the brink of faith, but only theology can explicate the meaning of a world informed by faith. We will examine this relation more adequately in a later section in philosophical theology, as it relates to a doctrine of man. But this section makes it clear that Macquarrie is willing to go so far as to "secularize" such terms as "grace" and "creation" in order to capture a meaning in our experience of Being which is common to all persons but usually overlooked in characterizing Being: the experience of joy and the search for wholeness. Macquarrie sees these experiences as pointing to an understanding of Being in terms of a source of joy, unity, stability, wholeness. He is, in short, willing to draw the ontological implications of such experiences, claiming for them the same validity that Heidegger claimed for the experience of anxiety. His characterization of Being, even in its most secular form and apart from any incursion from Christian theology, seems to demand a language similar to that of religion. In order to keep the language purely philosophical, however, any religious terms borrowed for this fuller explication of the meaning of Being must reduce the scope of their reference to the common experience of Being and avoid planting a specifically religious meaning to human experiences. Macquarrie does believe, of course, that human experience has a religious dimension. But, *qua* philosopher, he uses religious terminology in his description of joy and wholeness only in a reduced form which prevents them from importing specific ideas or doctrines of religious faith. The terms "grace", "creation", "wholeness", and "Holiness" are used, then, to give a proper description of Being as "letting-be", a description that must take into account those positive "being-ful" experiences of man that easily lead him to religious faith.

The significance of such a move is immediately obvious. The Christian is already supplied with a host of important terms which need only the added element of faith in order to become theological. Terms which were once meaningful only within the domain of Christian faith have found a meaning grounded in common human experience, a meaning that at once rightly describes real aspects of human experience and opens toward a world of meaning inside Christian faith.

The development of a philosophy that leads to the brink of faith and even provides experiential meanings for terms of Christian theology is tied to the three important aspects of Macquarrie's philosophy: an existential grounding, the phenomenological method, and the pursuit of ontological understanding. We have already seen how existentialism provides a means for understanding Being in terms of the human needs to *become* and to *understand* and have noted that Christian faith needs such philosophical underpinnings in order to comprehend the search for God. Now we see that a method of thought which relies on a description of human experience, apart from whatever presuppositions, interpretations, and prejudices may attend our experiences, allows us to describe the structures of Being in terms of the phenomena as they present themselves. We do not have to judge what is objective and what is subjective, what is fact and what is value, etc. We accept the phenomena as they present themselves, as structures of meaning in the world in which we live, including the moods which are so instrumental in disclosing these structures. And so we are able to see joy as well as despair and the need for wholeness, unity, and stability as well as the forces which fragment us. A descriptive analysis of human experience, a phenomenology of it, leads us to grasp structures of meaning that can be understood only in terms of an ontology, an understanding of Being, that gives these structures their validity as insights into Being. Thus, joy and wholeness come to be seen as comprehensible only in terms of an understanding of Being which establishes them as ontological possibilities.

Language

The purpose of this chapter is to explore Macquarrie's philosophy of language with the aim of discovering the inherent limits of the existential approach as applied to language. It aims specifically at delineating more precisely than was possible in the section on phenomenological ontology the nature of the third level of *aletheia*, which Macquarrie terms "God-talk".

We will begin with a discussion of Macquarrie's general philosophy of language. We can then proceed to see how he applies this philosophy to "God-talk" and other aspects of theological language which rely on the third level of *aletheia*. Finally, we can examine how mystery and paradox function within philosophical and theological language.

Macquarrie immediately and unequivocally separates himself from the tradition of contemporary British language analysts when he asserts that language cannot be considered as though it were an entity in itself. Language never exists "in itself" in the sense in which many analysts would like to imagine: as a structured reality composed solely of its own rules and bearing concrete reference to nothing but itself. Instead, Macquarrie views language as a "precipitate" of the "discourse situation": It always involves an attempt on the part of someone to use language to say something to someone. Language has life only in a discourse situation; it is the focus and the bearer of what is going on in that situation. Cut off from the discourse-situation, language is just an abstraction.[1]

One might say that the discourse situation is the "home" of language. This metaphor implies that the situation is much more than language, as it provides the context in which it can live. The discourse-situation is, in general, the total context of human life. This life is something that is partly public and partly transcendent of the particular situation, with the result that what is said might bear meanings that are not intended by the speaker (at least not explicitly intended). Thus, misunderstanding and misinterpretation become possible, requiring an analysis which *preserves* rather than disconnects the life situation from what is said. Any other approach risks distortion of meaning.[2]

Macquarrie says the total discourse-situation involves an *a priori* structure of the person. Man has a potentiality for developing a particular language, a potentiality which Macquarrie calls "depth grammar".[3] Thus, although language is learned, the innate disposition for it makes the acquired knowledge of grammar, linguistic forms, etc., *tacit*. We experience life in a context of language in some primordial way without explicitly formulating its specific meanings. This is the sense in which Macquarrie says that we are first "addressed" by Being.[4]

The primordial discourse from which all other modes are derived is that which involves the basic human situation of being a self-in-the-world. In the most general terms, world and self constitute a discourse situation.[5] Since discourse both unites and separates the speaker in respect to both the person addressed and the reality spoken about, it acts as a mediator between them. Its capacity to do this is grounded in what Macquarrie, following the notion of a Kantian *Anschauung*, calls "intuition". We have an intuitive grasp on reality through the structures of language. Intuition remains blind without language, but it is only man's being-in-the-world (to which we must point by extralinguistic means) that gives him something to talk about. "Intuition", however, means for Macquarrie far more than sense perception. Macquarrie extends its meanings to affective states as well, such as the state of anxiety. Thus, intuition discloses structures of existence in the world and, transcending sense-intuitions, have to do with "total existence" in which both subject and object are encompassed in one vision.[6]

Language provides the explicit context in which we carry on the business of life. It is not the measure of what can be thought but aids us in producing rational structures of expression: "Rationality needs language, but language is broader than rationality and corresponds to the whole range of personal being".[7] Word and idea have a *reciprocal* relation: they each have a measure of independence with which they can affect each other.[8]

Language reflects, more than anything else, the nature of human life as personal and communal. Indeed, the purpose of expression and representation is communication.[9] Discourse always involves an address to someone else:[10] "Communication takes place when some aspect of the shared world is lit up and made accessible to both parties in the discourse".[11] All communication is interpretation which takes place in a community of interpretation, and this implies a shared world, shared interests, and a shared universe of discourse,[12] discourse which bears a creative relation to the speakers who employ it and the world in which they live.[13]

The "seed" notion of language which Macquarrie espouses, then, is the idea that language is grounded in human life and that it cannot be separated or abstracted from it. It is certainly produced out of the *a priori* conditions of human existence, but it is not reducible to these conditions.[14] Language has a measure of independence and has the power to let Being address us; but it is a human structure and is entirely modifiable by human use. Language and thought, language and reality, language and life, etc., are in irreducible relationship with each other.

This fundamental fact concerning language leads Macquarrie to follow Wittgenstein in his notion of "language-games". Just as human life is lived out under a variety of conditions, situations, purposes, etc., so the language which is employed in these various circumstances shows marked differences. Indeed, the means by which one is able to speak about one thing may be completely inadequate for speaking about another. Entire areas of a life may be nearly independent from the experiences of another.[15] Language can be understood only when placed in the context of the situation in which it arises.[16] Its "logic" is not composed merely of the relation of words and sentences but of their "place" or "home" in the community of discourse.[17] Each "home" is a center around which the meanings of a group of life experiences and activities gravitate to form a quasi-independent language or "game" of language[18] which has its own logic and its own criteria for meaning and truth.[19] Saying that every language has its own logic is not, of course, to say that they are equally valuable or useful or that some of them may not be illusory or misleading. We must investigate the particular language to discover its worth. This applies particularly to situations in which two different accounts from two different perspectives (eg., the theological and the scientific) are in genuine tension with each other.[20] For no one language-game is reducible to another, nor is it desirable that it should be so.[21]

The notion of language-games is one which Macquarrie does not develop strongly in his philosophy of language, and it has had little effect on the rest of his philosophy and theology. I suspect that this is the case because it is a rudimentary exploration of a concept that moves in a different direction from the tenor of his work. But it is an important notion because it contains the seed of a solution to the paradoxes represented by the limits of an existential approach to philosophy and theology. Certainly, if Macquarrie argues that no one language-game is reducible to another, one wonders why he wishes to unite anthropological, cosmological, and theological langauge in one ontological language-game! If he wishes to follow Wittgenstein in his use of the term "language-game", no "universal" meaning of the word "Being" seems possible. And it is precisely his attempt to effect such a universal meaning for Being that is responsible for the limits of existential language for referring meaningfully to historical and scientific facts, which might be considered to pertain to their own language-games. Because Macquarrie does not take seriously enought the import of what he says concerning language-games, he creates an existential-ontological language which, though it has its own function and validity, is put forward as the "depth meaning" implied in other language-games dealing with man, the nature of the world, and God. We will reconsider this undeveloped aspect of Macquarrie's philosophy in the conclusion of this work in the context of a concept of "domains" of knowledge, since it holds some promise as a means of breaking out of existential theology toward a mode of thought in which other language-games play an essential role. I will argue that each domain is a kind of "language-game" which obeys its own rules and criteria of meaning while being "open" (like a family member) to the assertions of other domains.

But at this point we must return to an analysis of Macquarrie's philosophy of language. *Meaning*, for Macquarrie, is a much broader notion than that which ties it to the meaning of words. Single words are not devoid of meaning,[22] but their meanings do not necessarily correspond to the meaning they have in sentences.[23] The former is an abstraction of the latter.[24] Meanings are fluid and changeable, dependent upon context and "language-game". Further, the connotative power of a word may import meanings which intensify or create complexities in its meaning. Connotations provide the interpretive capacity, its power to light up meaning, which Macquarrie considers quite different from its power to refer to objects.[25]

This notion of connotation will be expanded in Macquarrie's concept of a symbol, which will be discussed at length later. It suffices for now to note that words function to express meaning in many ways, connotation being a very important bearer of meaning. For connotations involve the expression of the experience, the personal dimension, out of which the speaker communicates.

Macquarrie distinguishes a number of functions which language performs. First, it expresses the human being himself (thus making connotation an important bearer of meaning). Language is our opening to the world and to others. Our whole world, even the world of perception, is personalized in language, organized by the personal knower. It expresses life and reality in such a profound way that no "objective, constructed" language can ever capture the true expression of language.[26]

Secondly, language *refers*: it is directed at some reality it wants to express. It isolates and brings into focus particular elements from the undifferentiated background of entities of which we are aware. It lights up what we are talking about[27] and brings it into the focus of attention. Macquarrie does not identify "referring" with "picturing", claiming that the latter lacks the dynamic of the former. The reference is always beyond the subjectivity of the referrer and involves symbols, metaphors, analogies, etc. In bringing the hiddenness of Being to light, language brings about *aletheia*.[28] Thus, Macquarrie seems to make *altheia* an "object" of reference and to collapse the distinction between the connotative "subjective" and emotive modes of *aletheia* and the factual "objective" modes.

Some clarification of this apparent ambiguity lies in Macquarrie's concept of representation. He says that the link between language and reality is representation. Even analogy and symbolic language refer by means of representing what is experienced. But some modes of representation are more abstract and "objective", while others are more "self-involved", or "subjective". In any case, language re-presents what it talks about.[29]

A third function of language may be mentioned in this context: language *articulates* reality. I.e., it unifies areas of experience into coherent wholes;[30] it gives shape to the world and allows us to find our way around in it.[31] A sense of self-hood (egoity), social cohesion, the idea of an ordered world, etc., all depend upon this function of language. This does not mean that the articulated world is the mere product of an imaginative, creative linguistic act; rather, language articulates the very nature of things, making the unities of reality accessible to man.[32]

Representation, then, appears to be the referential mode of language. It cannot be identified with language which speaks "objectively", describing reality in its factual modes, nor can it be identified with language which reveals the personal, "subjective" dimensions of experience and consciousness. Language, Macquarrie says, articulates reality. It reveals Being. But what it reveals of Being must either be *other* than what either "subjective" or "objective" modes of language reveal, or else it must somehow include them while transcending both. Macquarrie appears to want to opt for the latter of these two possibilities. The issue that must be raised at this point, however, concerns the status of the language about Being. Once both subjective and objective modes are transcended, what can we *say* about what language reveals? When we say that language articulates reality, that it reveals it on some level "above" the mode of factual description, we seem to slip precisely into this mode, imagining to ourselves (or "representing") a normally invisible superstructure of Being upon which the experienceable facts of the world hang. We seem only to shift from a more superficial language about the nature of things to a more profound one which reveals something of the conditions of the former. In this sense, the transcendence of the objective mode may be measured by the *scope* of our reference rather than by a qualitative change of it. Thus, one cannot say properly that one has avoided "objectivity" in one's language about Being. Yet this is in a sense what Macquarrie wishes to say; and his wish, which is grounded in a belief that factual description can be only a secondary and derivative langauge that is grounded in a language which grasps the primordial event of human-being, is contradicted by a claim of objectivity for this revelatory language, which must be forwarded over against an accusation of its subjectivity. Macquarrie does not adequately distinguish between the sort of objectivity that applies to the language which reveals Being and the secondary and derived language which describes factual states. The ambiguity which results accounts to a considerable degree for his assertion that scientific and historical facts are essential to theology while, at the same time, denying their value by defining such facts as incapable of either establishing or disestablishing faith. He further undercuts their importance by claiming that attempts to establish historical or cosmological facts in relation to theology are generally "speculative" and without any essential value to Christian faith. That he doesn't wish to *ground* Christian faith in factual language is understandable, since obviously the language of faith must somehow reveal the human dimension of the believer's relationship with a personal God; but that this language should claim an objectivity which makes irrelevant any *concrete* reference to reality in terms of what Macquarrie calls a secondary and derived factual language is to separate illegitimately what must remain connected, even if this connection, the inherent connection between *factual* reality and the broad descriptive structures of Being, is a difficult one to articulate. It ends up by making of theology a private language which dares to speak only to its own circle of friends, inaccessible for evaluation and critique by those, informed by factual dimensions of language, who want to understand what theology *says*. Theology, under the influence of existential-ontological language, withdraws from a spiritual encounter with the normal, everyday world, making its language into an esoteric reference to a reality marked "for believers only". It loses its evangelical power.

Fourth, language has the function of *communicating* to others what is being said. It provides a matrix of common sharing wherein the transmission of ideas, thoughts, feelings, etc., becomes possible. Communication extends sharing, shares illumination in many areas: values, beliefs, ideas, interests, etc.[33]

Fifth, language has a *creative* function: it can create new thought. Language and thought are not identical, even if thought can be expressed only in language; so thought can be creatively influenced by the language in which it is couched. It evokes new awareness, which, in turn, uses language in a new and imaginative way, producing new forms and new symbols.[34] Macquarrie says that language is an emergent phenomenon. It appears with qualitatively novel unities of articulation which are not explicable simply in terms of the antecedent elements out of which it has arisen. If the "germ" of the emergent characteristic is in some sense already in the antedent elements, it can be seen only in retrospect of the emergent quality. The "higher" language cannot be understood in terms of the lower, and one can see the potential for it in the lower only from the vantage point of the higher language.[35]

These five functions of language point at once to the inherent ambiguities of Macquarrie's notion that language can represent Being in some way and to a solution to these ambiguities. The prime ambiguity, as we have seen, lies in Macquarrie's insistence that language can represent Being while escaping an objective, factual description of it as well as a subjective, emotive limitation. Language can say something about Being without recourse to the limitations of factual language or of emotive language, even if it uses these secondary and derivative forms as material for the metaphors, symbols, etc., which can open us to Being. The problem lies in the fact that this language does not easily refer back to factual and emotive language, such that the sciences, history, psychology, anthropology, ethics, political and economic domains of knowledge, etc., are properly grounded in it. While it claims to say something objective about Being, it denies to itself the forms of factual objectivity which pertain to these latter forms of knowledge as valid for its own form. And while this may be correct concerning itself and the religious language it claims to open up to us, it is not correct to say that other language-games are not essentially relevant to the religious and existential-ontological one. In doing so, Macquarrie hopes to avoid the critique which science can level at religious language. But his success in avoiding such a critique has made it impossible to assert factually the sorts of things that Christians ought to assert: e.g., the resurrection. Thus, these things have to be interpreted in a Bultmannian fashion, even while Macquarrie insists that some sort of factual reality, which must remain unspoken for fear of engaging in illegitimate speculation, pertains to such things. And worse, he withdraws religious language from an active, dialectical encounter with other domains of knowledge which rely more heavily on factual forms of language, much weakening the capacity of Christianity to speak to the concerns of the world.

The solution to these difficulties lies in Macquarrie's notion that the various language-games are involved in an *emergent* development in which one might easily suppose that two very different language-games, coming into close conjunction around a single problem or issue for thought, might creatively evoke novel forms of language which transcend the limitations of the forms that compose it. Macquarrie does not develop this theme in relation to religious language, certainly not in regard to a solution to the problem which existential-ontological language presents when it is used as a primary model for religious language. Much more will be said for the development of this theme when I present my own theory of the religious "domain" of knowledge.

We can clarify the fundamental problem in Macquarrie's theory of language by analyzing more concretely what he means by "existential-ontological language" and by seeing how this is expanded into symbolic language, opening on religious language.

Macquarrie locates the justification for adopting an existential view of language in the nature of human existence itself. Man, as existence, is a self-transcendent being; thus, since man expresses *himself* in language, his language must express his going beyond the limits of any given state.[36] This basic existential insight into the nature of language must precede the sort of linguistic analysis that is commonly identified with philosophy in Britain and America. For this latter approach seems to consider words and sentences as "quasi-substantial ghostly entities that somehow get along by themselves and can be considered in complete abstraction from the people who express *themselves* in these words and sentences".[37] Existential analysis must precede linguistic analysis in the sense that it considers the *personal* use of words and sentences before resorting to an analysis of the linguistic structure of the usage abstracted from life-contexts.[38]

Macquarrie considers that Heidegger's language about Being provides us with a paradigm for escaping the subjectivism of which an existential approach might be accused. Employing Heidegger's concept of language and the existential analysis with which he approaches the notion of Being, Macquarrie hopes to provide us with a means for illuminating revelation, finitude, guilt, sin, and God from within the human situation. For these categories correspond to modes of human being, to universal structures which always pertain to the human context. Thus, Macquarrie wishes to converge existential and ontological language into theological language, where God is Being and the *summum bonum*. Religion is constituted by the convergence of these two languages.[39]

Thus, Macquarrie can begin by noting that, in many languages, "saying" is connected to words for "seeing" and "light", so that "saying" is an act whereby something is brought into the light, made to stand out from the undifferentiated background of all that may be vaguely present to our minds. "Saying brings thing into unhiddenness; it uncovers them (*aletheia*) so that we can "see" them.[40] What comes to light, of course, is not the nature of the particular being so much as Being itself. We can use the language which talks about particular beings in order to refer to being precisely because Being is present and manifest in beings, which convey through themselves insight into Being.[41] The ultimate referent of language, even when it is used to speak of particular beings of everyday, ordinary experience, is Being. And our insights into Being can be expressed in language that is not empty nor reducible to logical operators. The ultimate meaning of this language can be expressed best in theological terms.[42]

But on what is this theological language grounded? Does language convey us to insights into the very nature of God and Being? Macquarrie would give a very qualified "yes" to this question:

> Certainly we can never talk of it (being) as we do of persons or things. We can never talk of it in itself . . . We ourselves are, and only on the basis of its self-giving and self-disclosing to us can we know it. Thus if we say anything about being, we are also saying something about ourselves. Talk of being, however it may express itself grammatically, is neither subjective nor objective talking, but holds these two together. So it must be repeated that it is not metaphysical talk, since this tries to take being . . . for the object of a rational investigation.[43]

Macquarrie's answer seems to be that the existential-ontological refers to Being only in so far as it illuminates the human situation, not as a mere subjective grasp of fleeting states of being but as the fundamental structure of human existence. He claims that this is not metaphysical knowledge because it is not the result—and can never be the result—of a rational investigation. Here he intends to define a phenomenological-existential approach as nonrational, since it brings to light structures which reason cannot construct through its own exercise. But one can also assume that Macquarrie discounts metaphysics, considered as statements about Being as it is in itself, precisely because language never uncovers anything except the ontological-existential structure of human existence.

How, then, does language manage to transcend this difficulty so that, while escaping the charge of engaging in metaphysics, it can refer meaningfully to Being precisely in the sense in which Christians demand to speak: i.e., as God? Macquarrie introduces here the notion of *symbols*. Caught between the two notions that language need not be "clear" in the sense of indicating things in a definite and unambiguous manner[44] and that, nonetheless, language must justify its claim to the appropriate application of theology,[45] Macquarrie wishes to provide a means for language to speak meaningfully of being as God and not merely as the ground of human existence, in the sense of a "horizon" for interpreting human existence. Thus, he makes existential-ontological language serve as an interpretive parallel for the symbolic language involved in revelation.[46] Existential-ontological language helps us understand symbols, and symbols help to vivify and concretize the former.[47] Macquarrie asserts, then, that though the language of existence and being is the basic logic of theology, it must include images and symbols which, together with this language of existence, comes as close as possible to universality.[48] He says that the universal language about God and Being which develops from this interplay of language may allow us to speak about the world, the cosmos, with the same structure by which we describe the structures of human existence.[49] But it is difficult to tell whether Macquarrie is saying here that we can at last engage in metaphysical assertions about the cosmos based on symbols generated from existential-ontological language. If Macquarrie denies the validity of the universal ontological talk which is properly called metaphysics, what status does this cosmological language have?

We may now enter into an analysis of what Macquarrie means by "symbols" and how they open us to the Being which theology describes. First, we may clarify the meanings of some important words connected to symbols. An *image*, e.g., is a generic term that covers any kind of pictorial language. An *analogy* is not a mere picture, however; it depends on some intrinsic likeness between the analogue and that for which it stands and is a self-interpreting relation (e.g., God as "Father"). But a symbol does not require this sort of likeness to be effective. Rather, it participates in that which it symbolizes. A symbol (model, "cipher") stands for something that is in itself quite incomprehensible yet somehow gives us a way of coming to terms with the mystery.[50] It seems to be the same as a sign: "A sign is something public and manifest, yet something which always points beyond itself to what it signifies".[51]

The symbol lights up levels of meaning and of reality in ways conceptual language cannot do, even if it does require conceptual elucidation.[52] It is an intermediary between language and its ultimate referend.[53] Defining it perhaps too broadly, Macquarrie says, "in the widest sense of the word, a 'symbol' is anything which is presented to the mind as standing for something else".[54] In religion, symbols function in ways similar to literary metaphors. A response of feeling, specifically those feelings associated with a sense of the numinous, is involved; but so is insight into the cognitive dimension opened up by symbols, which also elicit from us a response of commitment to what is felt and known through them.[55] Symbol is language in which the words do not directly refer but "bounce off" what they refer to in order to illumine a more remote subject matter to which the speaker really wishes to refer.[56] They have Being present and manifest in them and throw light on actual structures.[57]

Anything can become a symbol for Being; but symbols are not arbitrarily chosen.[58] Indeed, Being actually takes the initiative in forming symbols:

> While the symbols are partly determined by the circumstances of the culture within which they function as symbols of Being, they are surely in part also determined by the initiative of Being in the revelation, for it is in and through these particular symbols that Being declares and manifests itself.[59]

Some symbols are more adequate than others. Their adequacy depends on how well they light up Being, and this is turn is determined by the range of participation in Being evidenced by that which serves as symbol. Macquarrie says that symbols may be ordered in the rank of a "hierarchy of beings": the higher the grade of being symbolized, the more adequate the symbol for revealing Being, since higher beings not only *are*, but they participate in the act of "letting-be", which is the key concept of Being.[60] Though Macquarrie distinguishes between intrinsic symbols, which have some sort of kinship what they symbolize,[61] and conventional symbols, which are created by arbitrary choice[62] and have no intrinsic connection with what they symbolize, he does not seem to think that this distinction itself demarcates more adequate from less adequate symbols. Both types of symbols can fail by veiling themselves in an obscurity that necessitates reinterpretation and refurbishing in a manner similar to myth, thus ending up to be empty symbols. They are successful only while they successfully point to the reality they symbolize and relate that reality to our human existence.[63] There are no clear rules for the development of a symbol, which is affected even by the psychological differences of the individuals who create it or use it.[64] They develop within the life of a people and may develop out of anything in that life: a natural event, nature itself, some great experience of deliverance, etc. They have varying degrees of adequacy, varying potentialities for development, may be relatively fixed, or may change or die.[65]

Symbols seem to be a necessary part of language, since it is the most adequate means by which we can refer ultimately to the Being which initiates its own manifestation in the beings we more easily speak of. But they are not always readily comprehensible in ordinary language, perhaps because they do not refer to the ordinary. They often need to be comprehended in terms other than their own. Macquarrie says that existential-ontological language performs this function. As the most widely shared and communicable language, it can throw light on the meaning and use of symbol. In turn, symbol can illumine existential language. There is a relationship of reciprocal illumination between them.[66]

This reciprocal illumination functions by means of our capacity to use existential-ontological language in order to discover the structure of analogy which enables a symbol to reveal Being. Symbols illumine Being in terms of the similarity of relation obtaining between two beings and that between Being and beings: x is to X as x is to y. That is, a relation between two beings, acting in tandem as symbol, may be similar to the relation of a being to Being. This is an analogy which does not disclose Being as it is in itself but rather as it is *related* to us; and this latter relation can be illumined in existential-ontological language.[67]

Analogical language[68] is essential for understanding what religious language refers to and how it functions. We can, by demythologizing, translate mythical statements into existential-ontological ones. But we still must recognize the limit constituted by a transcendent God who is present and active in history. Since we cannot, Macquarrie says, use language to refer directly to this "limit" in an objective way any more than we can reduce it to specifically human or existential limits, we must use analogical language to refer to it.[69] Analogy is said to complete the existential significance of myth and symbol and is the natural way in which symbol finally expresses itself.[70] Symbol and the analogies we construct from them are our only way of referring to God, and we must be careful to use analogy in such a way that we do not anthropomorphize God or turn Him into mere myth. Macquarrie conceives analogy in such a way that God always "spills over" any reference that analogy can make to Him, so that He remains "radically other". It is this radical otherness of God, which remains undefined, which constitutes the limits of demythologization for Macquarrie. And in this sense the gospel cannot be "dekerygmatized".[71]

Analogies can be successful at accomplishing the task of developing a religious language because they do not "picture" realities. They are not "likenesses". Nor do they bog us down finally in a relation of participation between particular and universal. Instead, they manifest a relation more like the participation of an individual in community. In this sense, just as persons have an affinity for community and for language, one might say that man, the symbol-user, has an affinity for Being.[72] This affinity makes him the best material for symbols which refer to Being. Indeed, Macquarrie says that we clearly cannot apply our concepts of things analogically to a concept of God. The concepts which describe human existence are the proper source of analogies for God.[73] And the main reason for this is that man not only *is* but has the power to *let be*. He has a share in the creativity of God, who, as Being, creates by letting beings be. He is the condition of Being. And man himself shares in this kind of being in that he is creative, an "enabler-to-be", one who helps to fulfill the potentialities for being. In Macquarrie's view, this is the highest activity open for man and gives him an insight into the nature of *Agape*. Thus, man's creativity is a key analogy in any attempt to think of God, since creative, disinterested love is analogous to God's *Agape* as it lets-be beings.[74] Again, the temporal character of human existence is a key analogue for Being-God. Man does not simply persist through time from moment to moment. He transcends the kind of time objects have. He extends himself into the past, present, and future through memory, judgment, and anticipation, respectively; thus, he escapes mere successiveness. And this temporality serves as a fundamental analogue to the character of Being. It enables us, e.g., to see something of God's nature as acting in time while maintaining a stability in which past, present, and future are unified in the totality of his being. The temporal notion of selfhood, in which the self is time-transcending in the sense of being both stable and dynamic is the proper analogue for God.[75]

Despite the clear adequacy with which these analogies suggest themselves, Macquarrie insists that we keep in mind that such language is oblique and relatively inadequate, though the sufficient basis of "likeness"[76] allows us to use this language meaningfully. The incompleteness of such language allows us to view analogies, symbols, etc., as enhanced when they modify and correct each other. We can, e.g., understand something of the mystery of the incarnation in this way.[77] But, basically, analogies are not capable of yielding a direct conceptual knowledge of God.[78]

Clearly, Macquarrie's distinction between existential-ontological language and symbol as well as other non-religious language-games closely parallels the distinctions between the three levels of knowledge which we discovered in his epistemology. The first level, which includes the calculative thought and language, is a depersonalized language in which man does not express him*self*[79] *qua* language-user. Thus, "spiritual language" is distinguished from scientific and from "active-pragmatic" language-games.[80] The second level is represented by existential and ontological language, which illumines the structure and conditions of human existence. But this language cannot stand by itself, as perhaps, can the sciences, since it intends to talk about Being, which it cannot adequately do without reference to symbol, the third level of knowledge. It would seem that, since existential-ontological language is tied reciprocally to symbol, they must *together* constitute religious language, which has its own criteria of meaning and sense within the parameters of its "game". We can now turn to the question of the nature of religious language in order to see how this reciprocal relation unfolds an understanding of God.

Macquarrie does not try to "prove" the existence of God by recourse to the classical arguments for God's existence. Language itself reveals at least a necessity to speak of God: language universally contains God-talk and embraces a realm that transcends everyday phenomena. God is always there in language, indicating that the order of the universe which makes language possible and the fact of universal religious experience express His genuine reality in terms of God-talk.[81] "The fact that common patterns of talk may be seen in widely scattered faiths suggests that there is some universal logical structure that characterizes theological discourse".[82] "The very fact of language with its strong indications that its 'grammar' has its roots in a trans-human reality is evidence of an ordered universe, and this is part of what we mean when we speak of God".[83]

Macquarrie's remarks make it clear that religious faith is natural to man. Man is inherently already involved in an existential transcendence of which the ultimate reference is Being, which can be understood adequately only in religious language.

> ... faith is not primarily assent to propositions, but an existential attitude of acceptance and commitment; and that revelation is not primarily given in the form of statements, but it is rather the self-giving or self-communication of being. That which discloses itself in revelation seizes the whole being of man and cannot be adequately expressed within the limits of language.[84]

The revelation of Being cannot be mediated through ordinary language, even if ordinary language points inexorably to it. We must develop a religious language or, as in the case of Christianity, a theological language which acts as a vehicle for understanding and insight.[85], Thus, revelation becomes accessible through language, not simply as statements of fact, practical intention, or subjective emotion, nor as a doctrine or creed, but as a coming to light of *something*, of Being.[86] This means that, while avoiding any attempt to speak of God literally so as to make what is unique and incomparable into a finite being,[87] we must seek to show that revelation has some expressible content which the intellect can grasp.[88] Religious language must articulate in words what it claims to know, even if this involves stretching language beyond its normal usages in order to speak of God.[89] Religious language involves a cognitive content which seriously purports to say something meaningful[90] and which obeys rules. E.g., the predicates applied to God must follow a certain logic (God, e.g., cannot weigh a million tons). These rules may be pertinent only to theological discourse, but that discourse is itself justifiable as a necessary aspect or domain of our whole range of being-in-the-world in its cognitive, affective, and conative dimensions.[91] Macquarrie decries all forms of fideism and anti-intellectualism in religion, asserting that God-talk is not a self-justifying language.

The necessity of a language which refers ultimately to the ultimate, which discloses Being in its many manifestations in the context of human existence, is most firmly grounded in the context of human existence and in the natural human quest for grace. The word "God" has meaning as the correspondent of the experienced need for a grace which brings wholeness to what is always experienced as a somewhat fractured human existence. And if God has meaning as the answer to the question posed by human unwholeness, so too do words such as "finitude" (which means "creatureliness") and sin (separation from God).[92] Indeed, the Christian vocabulary expresses quite well the structure of human existence as it is perceived under sin and grace. The Christian message is distinct and cannot be told without a distinct vocabulary.[93] Some words may be, perhaps, changed for the better: "redemption" is perhaps better translated "liberation", even if the idea of payment is lost. And "justification" would be better translated "acceptance". But fundamental words like "sin", "faith", "grace", etc., cannot be translated out of Christian vocabulary.[94]

We can conclude this discussion with an analysis of the role of paradox and mystery in Macquarrie's thought. Without an understanding of these, it becomes difficult to grasp how symbols can refer to the infinite regions of being without contradiction of meaninglessness.

The infinity of Being is evident in man's transcendence. Man is called to transcend himself, to advance into a "beyond" consisting of a wisdom, goodness, love, etc., which, no matter how far one gets, still lies before one to enrich life. God is at the limit of these qualities in a "place" we cannot imagine but can point to—by analogy—when we say such things as "God is love". Such language can lead to paradoxes, such as when we say God is above the world and yet within it. But paradox is something that is expressed on a literal level and does not touch the deeper levels of thought.[95] Indeed, it enables us to see what is meant when language fails us otherwise.[96] This does not mean, of course, that paradox should be viewed as a means of clarifying difficult concepts. We should not plunge into paradox with the hope of inciting a fideist response of faith by virtue of deliberate obfuscation any more than we should avoid paradox by prematurely opting for one side or the other in a hurried way. We need to work out the genuine paradoxes that are unavoidable in Christian theology[97] and which make possible a grasp of the existential reality of Christianity.[98]

The questions raised by paradoxes are quite often mysteries, but they are not blank enigmas which are completely unanswerable. Mystery is a question in which we have glimpsed the shape and direction of an answer only to find that the more we penetrate into an answer, the more the horizons of the mystery expand so that we can never fully grasp them.[99] Mystery arises in situations in which the knower himself is involved so that he can never get total objectification. Mystery is inexhaustible. It does not contradict logic, though it does transcend it. It is neither absurd nor opaque but carries its own translucency to which we gain access by analogy, symbols, and the *via negativa*. Mystery is that "whither" of man toward which we transcend as we unfold the truth of total experience.[100]

When we "know" a mystery, we do not destroy its nature as mystery. We do not reduce it to a "clear and distinct idea", which is manipulable and remains at our disposal.[101] The prime focus of mystery is not nature (and certainly not mathematics) but persons. The being and interrelations of persons are inherently and infinitely mysterious. Thus, the affinity between the mystery of God and the mystery of man is especially important in the understanding of Christ, who manifests God in the flesh.[102]

Macquarrie does not deny that mysticism is an important and valuable mode of knowing for the Christian, though he does not identify it with the active, intellectual grasp of God that is represented in the on-going movement of the mind in touch with mystery. Mysticism contemplates in silence the transcendence that cannot be fully formulated. The mystic turns inward, finds the transcendence of which he is a part, and goes out beyond himself into that transcendence. If he wishes to articulate the mystery upon which he impinges, he must employ symbols, the *via negativa*, and silence.[103] But, *qua* mystic, he leaves the mystery unspoken, even without expression in paradox.

Being, which Macquarrie interprets in Christian symbolism as God, is the ultimate mystery. But even it is not a "blank incomprehensible". It is the condition that there may be beings. Thus, while we cannot say what it is, we must at the same time say that it is the most beingful.[104] Indeed, Macquarrie uses the word "metaphysical" and "mystery" interchangeably,[105] giving us insight into why he rejects metaphysics as a body of knowledge which can be stated in clear, descriptive language.

Notes

1. John Macquarrie, *God-Talk: An Examination of the Language and Logic of Theology* (London, 1967), pp. 65—67.

2. Ibid., pp. 65—67. Macquarrie is borrowing this term from Wittgenstein (Cf., *Philosophical Investigations*), asserting that this is the correct interpretation of what Wittgenstein means by "depth grammar".
4. John Macquarrie, *In Search of Humanity: A Theological and Philosophical Approach* (New York, 1983), pp. 98—99.
5. *God-Talk*, p. 69.
6. Ibid., pp. 75—76.
7. *Humanity*, p. 96.
8. John Macquarrie, *Thinking About God* (London, 1975), pp. 82—84.
9. *God-Talk*, p. 78.
10. Ibid., pp. 67—68. This is a fact which, when forgotten, leads to the depersonalization of language with consequent distortion of meaning.
11. Ibid., p. 74.
12. Ibid.
13. Ibid., p. 68.
14. The naturalistic account of language, such as that of Bertrand Russel, is inadequate because of its distorting reductionism. Such a theory attempts to show language to be a *physical* phenomenon (sounds, written pictures, etc.) which has its meaning in the effects or behaviour it causes. But this theory, Macquarrie says, fails to look beyond the physical substratum of language toward what is distinctive in language: its human aspect as a bearer of understanding and meaning. And the picture-theory of reality that attends this theory has no applicability beyond everyday perceptible facts. Besides this, Macquarrie asserts that words and sounds are not pictures, and they do not refer by picturing (*God-Talk*, p. 72). "Performative" language, e.g., brings about a new state of affairs and does not "picture" any aspect of reality (John Macquarrie, *Principles of Christian Theology* (London, 1977), p. 480). Not even modern physicists hold on to the picture-theory any more. The assumption here is that the real is the physical, and such reductionism in language renders language inadequate (*God-Talk*, pp. 57—59).
15. E.g., moral questions are quite different from questions concerning scientific fact or aesthetic questions.
16. *God-Talk*, p. 117.
17. *God-Talk*, p. 124.
18. The word "game" is intended by Wittgenstein to imply that the rules, logic, and purposes of one "area", "region", or "domain" of language are different from others.
19. *God-Talk*, pp. 111—114.
20. *Thinking About God*, pp. 4—5.
21. *God-Talk*, pp. 112—113. This is particularly the case with "person-language", which is a basic mode of discourse.
22. Ibid., p. 85. They have significance in the sense of "*Bedeutung*".
23. Ibid., p. 85. I.e., their *Sinn*.
24. Ibid., p. 85.
25. Ibid., p. 93. Assigning "meaning" to the connotation of a word seems an unfortunate consequence of an existential commitment. Macquarrie seems to say that the reference of a word denotes some particular object, situation, circumstance, etc., whereas the connotation reveals the meaning of what is denoted. Macquarrie says that the connotation and the reference of names are both equiprimordial

and that one may be more important than the other in certain contexts (*God-Talk*, p. 97). But when he says that connotations "light up meaning", it seems that he considers meaning to be something other than reference, an other that is more positive and valuable than reference. One can only suspect that he has in mind the revelation of structures of human existence which ground the fundamental life experiences of human being (*God-Talk*, pp. 89—90). Since meaning comes to light in connotation, it would appear that reference does not donate the positive value of meaning. This makes reference less valuable than connotation—or existential insight. Thus, "facts" lose their importance in existential analysis, which trades on the connotations of words.

26. *Humanity*, pp. 101—102.
27. In earlier works, Macquarrie reserves this role of "Lighting up" for connotation, whereas in a later work, he defines "reference" in terms of this role. This seems to be a genuine inconsistency, though it is a minor point. His view of linguistic meaning seems to be slightly vitiated by this ambiguous notion of reference. But, clearly, language remains the context in which Being reveals itself.
28. *Humanity*, pp. 102—103.
29. *God-Talk*, pp. 73—74.
30. *Humanity*, pp. 104—105.
31. *God-Talk*, pp. 73—74.
32. *Humanity*, pp. 104—105.
33. Ibid., pp. 103—105-
34. Ibid., p. 105.
35. *God-Talk*, p. 56.
36. John Macquarrie, *Existentialism* (Middlesex, England, 1972), p. 149.
37. John Macquarrie, *Twentieth-Century Religious Thought: the Frontiers of Philosophy and Theology, 1900—1960* (London, 12963), p. 317.
38. Ibid.
39. John Macquarrie, *Studies in Christian Existentialism* (London, 1966), pp. 94—95.
40. *God-Talk*, pp. 63—64.
41. *Principles*, p. 129.
42. Ibid., p. 128.
43. Ibid., p. 106.
44. *God-Talk*, pp. 114—115.
45. *Thinking About God*, pp. 6—7. Macquarrie, agreeing with David Pears (*Wittgenstein* (New York, 1971), p. 168) says that if the later Wittgenstein taught that there are no objective supports for language outside of human thought and language, so that meaning and necessity are preserved only in the linguistic practices that embody them, then theologians must part company with him and seek to give the credentials of their subject.
46. *Principles*, pp. 137 and 184.
47. Ibid., p. 184.
48. *God-Talk*, p. 239.
49. *Christian Existentialism*, p. 12.
50. *God-Talk*, pp. 196—199.
51. John Macquarrie, *The Faith of the People of God: A Lay Theology* (London, 1972), p. 75. We must note here that, although Macquarrie seems, as I stated earlier, to be influenced strongly by Tillich's notion of a symbol, his identification of a sign with a symbol is a clear departure from Tillich's own concept of

a symbol. For Tillich (*Dynamics of Faith*) distinguishes sharply between symbols and signs. I suspect that Macquarrie's commitment to Anglicanism, which describes the elements in the mass as "signs" of grace, may be influential in this identification.
52. *God-Talk*, p. 202.
53. *Principles*, p. 195. E.g., light has a nature which makes it possible to refer to Christ as the "light of the world".
54. Ibid.
55. *God-Talk*, p. 195.
56. *Principles*, pp. 134—135.
57. Ibid., pp. 178—179.
58. Ibid., pp. 143—144.
59. Ibid., 164.
60. Ibid., pp. 143—144 and *God-Talk*, p. 100.
61. *Principles*, pp. 135—136. Macquarrie himself says that this distinction is not clear-cut.
62. Ibid., p. 135.
63. *God-Talk*, p. 201.
64. *Principles*, p. 163.
65. Ibid., p. 163.
66. Ibid., p. 137.
67. Ibid., p. 139—141.
68. Symbols illumine Being by means of an analogy of the existential response which it evokes to a similar response evoked by the experience of the *Mysterium Fascinans*. The symbol cannot be reduced to the language which described the existential response, but being illumined by it, we can discover how the symbol refers to Being (*Principles*, p. 139). Symbols seem to be valid when they are seen in terms of the way they illumine Being as a prior enabling condition. Thus, we can justifiably say "God exists" in the sense that He is the *condition* of all being. So also we can say that He is Good, Wise, etc., in the sense that He is the condition of these in beings (*Principles*, p. 141).
69. John Macquarrie, *The Scope of Demythologizing: Bultmann and His Critics* (London, 1960), pp. 226—227.
70. *God-Talk*, pp. 214—216.
71. *Christian Existentialism*, pp. 161—163.
72. *God-Talk*, pp. 219—220.
73. *Twentieth Century Religious Thought*, p. 350.
74. *God-Talk*, pp. 224—225.
75. Ibid.
76. Macquarrie seems here to contradict his statements elsewhere that symbols are *not* likenesses (Cf., *God-Talk*, pp. 219—220).
77. *God-Talk*, p. 228.
78. Ibid., p. 218.
79. *The Scope of Demythologizing*, p. 197.
80. Macquarrie never clearly defines a language-game. One must suppose that here he is referring to large "families" of language-games. (Cf., *The Scope of Demythologizing*, p. 195).
81. *Humanity*, p. 101.
82. *God-Talk*, p. 31.
83. *Humanity*, p. 100.

84. *Principles*, p. 104.
85. Ibid., p. 127.
86. Ibid., pp. 105 and 127.
87. *The Faith of the People of God*, p. 43.
88. *Principles*, p. 105.
89. *God-Talk*, p. 27.
90. *God-Talk*, p. 110.
91. *God-Talk*, pp. 79—80.
92. *Christian Existentialism*, p. 9.
93. Ibid., p. 128.
94. Ibid., p. 129.
95. *The Faith of the People of God*, pp. 43—44.
96. *God-Talk*, p. 145.
97. *The Scope of Demythologizing*, p. 133.
98. Ibid., pp. 27—28. Some important paradoxes are represented by the following questions: How can the particular man manifest universal Being? How can the historical Jesus realize the ultimate possibility of existence? How could Jesus be the pre-existent, eternal Logos and the historical person? Was Jesus "adopted" as the son of God or was he God incarnate (Cf., *Principles*, pp. 306—310).
99. *Thinking About God*, p. 33.
100. Ibid., p. 42.
101. Ibid., p. 36.
102. Ibid., pp. 38—41.
103. Ibid., pp. 37—38.
104. *Principles*, p. 113.
105. John Macquarrie, *The Concept of Peace*, (London, 1973), p. 63.

Conclusion

We can now conclude this work by raising again the issues which have emerged as we have tried to delineate Macquarrie's philosophy and theology. We must ask whether and how much Macquarrie's work can engender a response to these issues and attempt to resolve them by preserving as much of Macquarrie's positive contributions as possible. I believe that the essential thrust and character of Macquarrie's work can be preserved as we embark on an adventure of thought which he hesitates to take in order to center his thinking around existential modes of philosophy. My suggested resolutions to his difficulties will act to limit the influence of existential and phenomenological thought in the theology we can derive from him, though it will by no means preclude it from having an active role in it. Though the following presents a different direction in theology from that which Macquarrie has taken thus far, I believe that it is not a direction that is unacceptable to him, especially since it tries to preserve his major insights while putting them in a clarified perspective in regard to each other.

The first problem that we take up deals with the question of truth. He has identified truth with *aletheia* and has identified *aletheia* with what is disclosed in existential-phenomenological analysis, an analysis that enters easily into ontology. Thus, *aletheia* refers to the various degrees of the disclosure of Being. But, if *aletheia* is the essential nature of truth, what word shall we apply to the kind of truth that is affirmed in the sciences and other areas of thought? How can we characterize these kinds of truth, which must be stated in ways which differ from the language of *aletheia*, even when the notion of *aletheia* is presupposed and included in them? Macquarrie seems to lose himself in this problem, sometimes strictly identifying truth with the *aletheia* that arises out of existential phenomenology and sometimes speaking of empirical facts as being somehow *in relation* to *aletheia*.

Related closely to this problem is his close identification of religious thought with the analogical and symbological developments of existential phenomenology. He slides so easily from the *aletheia* of existential-ontological knowledge into a Christian symbology of Being that the former can be viewed only as a *necessary* ground for what appear to be its mere extension in terms of Christian symbolism and analogy to the notion of a personal God. When we raise the question concerning the sort of truth that applies to the kinds of *facts* that seem relevant to Christian faith and theology, e.g., scientific and historical facts, we find Macquarrie acknowledging that they are relevant but giving little emphasis to their role in theological thinking. They are "interpreted" in terms of what they have to offer as forms of *aletheia*, and factual controversies are set aside as adventures of speculation. The historical claims of the Christian faith lose their historical reference and serve only to disclose Being in the context of existential-phenomenological analysis. But we must ask whether this is sacrificing too much of the actual claims Christians want to make. Can we not take Paul seriously when he says, "If Christ be not risen, then is our preaching vain, and your faith is also in vain" (I Corinthians 15:14, KJV)? Paul clearly meant this literally; and, even if we do not wish to accept without question the first century cosmology and myth in which Paul might also have believed, we cannot, as Macquarrie acknowledges, radically demythologize every claim of faith. If *something* happened in the historical realm to effect the reality of faith which we now possess, we are responsible as theologians only when we seek to disclose *what happened*; and that would seem to imply a genuine concern with historical truth in its factual mode.[1] And if we are required to seek historical truth, how much more are we required to speak to issues raised by scientific claims, many of which challenge the very grounds of Christian faith? Clearly, theology and religious thought in general seem to demand an explicit relationship to areas of knowledge which make factual claims as claims which differ in many respects from truth as an existential disclosure of Being.

In this vein, we must examine Macquarrie's works with an eye to clarifying the following notions: truth as *aletheia* and truth as *fact*, phenomenology, existentialism, existential phenomenology, existential ontology, phenomenological ontology, ontology, and metaphysics. A clarification of these terms will help to properly divide some of the issues we must raise in the context of Macquarrie's work and will serve to demonstrate some of the limits of Macquarrie's use of existential thought in theology. For then we can also clarify the role of analogy and symbol and determine their role not only within existential-phenomenological *aletheia* but also in the other domains of thought to which Macquarrie alludes.

We must then also take up the problem of the nature of at least some of the domains of knowledge that are relevant to religious thought, which must itself be clarified as a domain in its own right. We must clarify the relation of these domains to the concept of truth as *aletheia* and to the kinds of truth that each of them professes. And this will involve a further clarification of the nature and role of analogy and symbol in each domain; how does each domain contribute to a unified understanding of Being?

This question leads naturally to a need to further clarify the process of emergence which Macquarrie outlines as part of the ontology undergirding the natural sciences. Since he speaks of it as an ontology, then he locates this process in the very heart of Being; and we must, then, clarify how it pertains to some other domains of knowledge.

All of these problems and tasks which Macquarrie's philosophical theology has presented to us can, I maintain, be resolved at least to some degree by properly developing elements of his thought which remain undeveloped but which indicate directions in which his thought might legitimately flow. What follows is an attempt to apply a clarified perspective of Macquarrie's thought to his own problems.

We can begin by clarifying the way in which Macquarrie uses the key terms of the existential philosophy undergirding his theology. The word "existential", in its adjectival sense, refers to knowledge (as well as generally to philosophies) constituted by an analysis of human existence. It refers specifically to the structures of human existence which are disclosed in such analysis. In its nominal sense, which is derived directly from Heidegger, it refers to the broad categories which distinguish the structures of human existence from other ontological structures. "Phenomenology" refers to the descriptive process of disclosing the essential structures of any being or type of being; it is closely related to the word "ontological", which refers to the structures of being disclosed by the phenomenological method. Phenomenology considers these structures simply in the descriptive terms which delineate them; ontology relates these structures as being to other structures in order to build a wider concept of Being. "Phenomenological ontology" is an ontology grounded in the phenomenological method. "Existential ontology" is an ontology grounded in an analysis of the structures of human existence, which differ considerably from the structures of nature. It is generally also viewed as a form of phenomenological ontology which is applied to the structures of human existence. This is indicated more specifically by the term "existential phenomenology", which slides easily into existential ontology.

These terms may be viewed as part of the "family" of existential language. Existential language functions to distinguish between structures of human existence and those pertaining to natural being. It emphasizes the former and slides into an ontology based on existential analysis; but phenomenology is able to deal with natural being and construct an ontology on that basis as well. The word "metaphysics" has quite a different thrust, referring to a rational process of deducing structures of being from a more empirical base. Macquarrie generally disclaims metaphysics, asserting that it is an illegitimate ontology connected to the now surpassed naturalistic and idealist philosophies. He tends to identify truth as *aletheia*, which is a degree of disclosure of Being, though he also wishes to reserve a meaning which corresponds to the sort of truth that is empirically established. These terms are encountered often in his works, and I use them often in making key distinctions in this discussion of his works. I have clarified them in the sense in which I think he most consistently means to use them and in which I have used them to make distinctions and create various developments in his philosophical theology.

We can now proceed to set forth a new direction which Macquarrie's philosophy and theology is able to take in the interest of overcoming the difficulties of his present system. Thus far we have seen that Macquarrie leans very heavily on existential thought in the development of his own thought. Influenced heavily by Martin Heidegger, but also by the Thomistic tradition and the British empirical-analytic school of philosophy, Macquarrie develops an interpretation of Christian faith which seeks to integrate with greater clarity than existentialism usually affords a unity of Christian thought with existentialism. This integration has stressed a movement of thought from various areas of human experience, such as religion, science, and other domains of thought, toward a disclosure of Being as undergirding all of them. Thus, he has made the degrees of this disclosure (*aletheia*) the main concept of truth while being sensitive to an empirical notion of truth which he never successfully integrates into *aletheia*. And this failure has led to an uneasy identification of religious truth with *aletheia* and to a confused relationship of *aletheia* with empirical facts, such as are set forth in the sciences. The development of truth as *aletheia* has emphasized one direction of movement: from experience to "ground" of experience through phenomenological-existential analysis. The "ground" is understood as Being, grasped in various degrees and, with each degree, manifesting a higher unity of comprehension which undergirds all areas of knowledge and lends them a more explicit unity.

I have already noted that the main problem with this system, the main reason why it cannot in principle successfully speak of development toward any kind of total synthesis, which it seems to want to do, is that its notion of Being is developed in a uni-directional manner. We can move from particular experiences to a comprehension of Being; but we cannot move from a comprehension of Being to an adequate description of particular experiences. The particularity of experience possesses an irreducible contingency which is not presupposed in the phenomenological explication of being as we move to it from experience. Thus, the disclosure of the structure of Being is valid as we proceed in the direction of Being only and does not provide empirical, contingent knowledge when we attempt to reverse the direction of a phenomenological investigation by asking what may be said *empirically* about a phenomenon as an implication of the phenomenological disclosure of Being which it affords. These two different types of truth have remained immiscible in Macquarrie's philosophy.

I do not wish to argue, however, that, since a phenomenological approach fails to give us access to empirical truth as the scientist normally understands it, we ought to throw out phenomenology on the grounds that it is an idealism and ground theology firmly in the empirical sciences. My point here is not to establish a thoroughgoing empiricism in theology. For the truth of a domain *cannot* be grasped solely on empirical grounds as they are usually understood—and misunderstood—in the natural sciences. The tension which I have described as drawing the phenomenological-existential and empirical aspects of truth in each domain into an inescapable dialogue with each other *means* that Being cannot be understood on empirical grounds alone.

I propose that we understand *aletheia* as Macquarrie has done, as *degrees* of truth, but without identifying *aletheia* with the disclosure of Being in the context of phenomenological-existential analysis. I believe that Macquarrie would like to view truth as a comprehensive understanding of both the contingent world of experience *and* the unified structures of Being that they reveal; and I think it is possible, by breaking his identification of *aletheia* with truth, to find a relationship between empirical modes of knowledge and "*aletheia*" which indicates a notion of truth that more adequately includes both senses of truth which Macquarrie acknowledges. I would like to locate the thrust of the notion of truth more in the empirical mode as Macquarrie understands it (i.e., in its "broad" and "loose" sense) than in its phenomenological sense without sacrificing the unique understanding of truth which phenomenological-existential analysis provides. This represents a shift from Macquarrie's near identification of truth with *aletheia*, but it does not deny the meaning of truth which he applies to *aletheia*. I propose this shift because it represents a move back to a more normally accepted notion of truth: the truth is communicated in statements which tell us what is the case in the world. This implies a grasp of some sort of objective, if insensible reality which we might encounter in concrete ways. And this notion of truth seems more adequate *prima facie* than a notion in which truth is reduced to the *meaning* of experience as spelled out by essential structures of being which generate an ontology no longer touching the world in which we live.

We have already noted that the uni-directionality of the disclosure of Being creates a systematic structure of ontological understanding which "fractures" or "breaks" when we reverse the process to ask what empirical knowledge might be implied in the disclosure of Being. These breaks occur most dramatically along lines which demarcate entire regions or *domains* of knowledge. Thus, e.g., ethical or moral knowledge seems to break off in the direction of a pursuit of a type of understanding which is quite different from that of other domains like religion or science. I have chosen the word "domain" to indicate these major *types* of breaks in the system as we reverse phenomenological enquiry toward the particular, concrete, empirical experiences that ground it, because it signifies an area of human enquiry and knowledge that falls under the *governance* of a criterion that is unique as the means of judging truth *within* the domain. The fracture which signifies the existence of a domain of knowledge is not, however, without relation to the existential-ontological structures from which the domain separates itself. In the first place, the alethic relationship is kept intact: we may view the disclosure of Being which is established in phenomenological and existential analysis as "undergirding" or providing a foundation for other truth statements we might make under the governance of the particular domain's criteria. But, more important than this, is the relationship between concrete reality and possibility which obtains between the truth as established within the domain and the "alethic" aspect which undergirds it, respectively. The function of the search for truth *within* a domain is to establish what is objectively the case in the world *as viewed from within the domain and as judged by its own criteria*. This is a broadly empirical notion of truth (Cf., the discussion concerning what is "broadly empirical" in the section on "science"). But the function of the search for truth as the disclosure of the structures of Being that are manifested by phenomenological-existential analysis of the experiences of the world is different. Such content for analysis is generated by a domain's unique perspective, and it explicitates the *meaning* of these experiences by placing them in the context of a structure of Being in which they are seen as types of a range of *possible* experiences of Being. The grasp of structures of being which is yielded from phenomenological-existential analysis outlines the essential and ontological interconnections between types of beings, of which the concrete reality touched on in the particular experiences of any domain is only one, or else only a partial manifestation in the concrete world. The various possibilities of being and the deeper interconnections of the being that is concretely manifested are all *possible* directions for investigation within the domain. They are not revealed in the domain itself until phenomenological-existential analysis unfolds the meaning of an experience which suggests these deeper aspects of the experience itself.

I am identifying "meaning" here with a *deepening* and *widening* of the scope of knowledge represented by concrete experience within a domain. Such experience "means" or "points to" deeper dimensions of experience and knowledge within the domain. Until the *possibilities* of such development within the domain are revealed by phenomenological-existential analysis, we cannot easily develop any knowledge within the domain. The "undergirding" which *aletheia* offers each domain is the ultimate meaning to which knowledge in any domain points. The truth of a domain is not to be located solely in this meaning nor solely in the empirical investigations carried out within the domain, but in the total grasp of the nature of concrete reality in the context of the contributing perspectives within each domain, as developed by an ongoing task of *reciprocal* enhancement of both aspects of truth.

The empirical aspect of truth within a domain and the alethic dimension of truth are *interdependent*. Without concrete experience within a domain, phenomenology and existential analysis have no material with which to disclose Being. But, when such disclosure is present (as it always is to some extent), it lights up *possibilities* for both investigation and development of concrete knowledge and experience which would otherwise languish for lack of direction and promise. Both aspects of the development of truth constantly interplay to confirm, correct, enhance and enrich, disconfirm and reject, etc., what is held to be true in each aspect. Their connection "across the break" is strong enough to define them as different functions or methodologies within a "synthetic" definition of truth. Truth is "synthetic" in that it is a synthesis of empirical experience of concrete reality and its phenomenologically disclosed meanings: i.e., it is a synthesis of the facts of concrete reality and meaning. This synthesis is a grasp of Being from the perspective of a "higher" unity between concrete reality and meaning. The statement of these unities depends upon the exercise of a "language-game" that can properly obey rules of language unique to the domain in which it is based and which can be flexible and creative enough to generate new rules and manifest new perspectives. The word "synthesis" refers broadly to the new unity effected by a new level of insight, which is generated by the interplay of alethic and empirical truth. How this movement of man's knowing and being attains "higher" levels is best described in the contexts of the domains I have focussed on in this work: science, history, and religion. There are other domains as well, such as economics, philosophy as a subject matter, political and social thought, ethics, etc., but an explicitation of these would take us far from the scope of this work.

Each domain, then, is a broadly empirically grounded region of knowledge which is governed by criteria for truth that are unique to it. The domain cannot progress to any radically new discovery, conceived as genuine "paradigm shifts", without an interplaying relationship with an alethic aspect of truth, which sets the ultimate limits of what can be thought in any domain. It burgeons with a surplus of meaning in the form of possibilities of being which, once outlined by the imaginative and linguistically creative phenomenological-existential analysis that is at the root of such knowledge, suggest routes to new discovery in the particular domains. And, as we pursue these routes, our focus on the concrete leads us into a "surplus" of experience which spills over into an explicitation through phenomenological-existential analysis. Each aspect of the process of discovering truth carries its own surplus of experience or meaning which demands treatment by the other aspect. They "energize" each other as long as we have a fundamental commitment to seek for truth. Thus, the system of meaning-grounding and deepening in any domain of knowledge grows and modifies with each new synthesis, as does the domain itself. Each synthesis grows out of the "promise" that is resident in each aspect of truth as this process moves back and forth across the "break" that establishes the particular domain. There is a temptation to call this a "dialectical" relationship; but this term bears with it too many unwanted Hegelian and Marxist connotations. Further it implies a duality of relation between "opposites"; and I do not envision these aspects of truth as having an "opposing" relationship. Moreover, as we shall soon see, the duality of this relationship is surpassed by the coincident relationship between the alethic aspect of truth and in any one particular domain and that which simultaneously pertains to *all* other domains of knowledge; and this more complex notion of interplay becomes even more very complex when we consider that each domain is in similar relationship with the truth of other domains! I prefer instead to refer to this relationship, both that between the alethic aspect of truth and the empirical aspect of truth *within* a particular domain as well as the relationship between the different types of truth in the various domains themselves, which actually involves a complex interrelationship of *both* aspects of truth in one domain with those of the other, a *mutually corrective or confirming cross-referencing relationship*. This is rather a mouthful and can be signified by the shorter phrases which suggest the whole, such as "the cross-referencing relationship" or the "mutually corrective" one, or even "mutually corrective synthesis".

We must note one subtle difference, however, between the mutually corrective synthesis which occurs between the empirical aspect of a domain and its alethic process and that which obtains between these various syntheses of interplaying domains. In the former, the cross-referencing activity passes back and forth across a "break" which divides two aspects of a form of truth that is relatively homogeneous throughout. E.g., the phenomenological-existential analysis that uncovers *types* of religious experience and life, thus manifesting various possible structures and modes of religious life, uncovers truth that is homogenous in type with the concrete, empirical experiences that it depends on. The mutual correction and confirmation that occurs in the cross-referencing activity is kept "in the family". The correction and confirmation has more the character of avoiding mistakes and illegitimate ways of thinking *within* the domain than it has of "testing out" a notion that seems somehow foreign. When we apply the cross-referencing activity to the different types of truth represented by *different* domains, however, the ideas of one domain can be quite foreign to those of another. There may be no way to understand them at all in the context of a domain that is foreign to them; or else they may engender a new comprehension of *both* domains. The ideas of one domain, when cross-referenced to another, can act to form a new synthesis of conceptuality. And this synthesis can, in turn, be "profundized" by the application of phenomenological-existential analysis to the experience to which the conceptuality refers. Such cross-referencing may, however, engender a conflict of ideas in which one domain or the other must modify itself by retreating from at least some aspect of its assertion of truth. Perhaps a whole domain will collapse. In any case, the cross-referencing of domains of knowledge is essential to the development of syntheses which point to a total, broadly empirical truth concerning the nature of reality as a whole. Our attainment of higher levels of knowledge depends upon the achievement of both of these types of synthesis.

In the light of this distinction between the kinds of cross-referencing that pertain to the two different areas of activity, that *within* a domain and that *between* domains, it seems helpful to refer to these different areas by different names. The problem presented by any attempt to do so, however, is that one is likely to obscure the essential truth that cross-referencing goes on *both* within and between domains. The search for a different name for either the *inner domainic or inter* domainic cross-referencing activity can easily end up settling for merely different words which lose some of the essential meaning that they are supposed to convey. I propose, in this case, to define what goes on both *within* and *between* (or among) domains as the cross-referencing activity that I have described.

But these different areas of activity can be given some clarifying descriptive designations. In the case of the cross-referencing activity that goes on *within* a domain, we can refer to an *inner, tensional* cross-referencing activity. The word "inner" here has an obvious meaning, as it refers to what goes on only within a specific domain of knowledge under the governance of rules of language and criteria for "rightness" that are unique to it. The word "tensional" here refers to the much tighter relation that obtains between the two *aspects* of truth in a single domain, the *alethic* and the empirical.

To clarify this "tensional" concept of interrelation between *alethic* and empirical aspects of truth, we must be reminded here that *all* acts of knowing and *every* knowledge claim involve assertions that are *at once* empirical and "ontological-existential" (or, *alethic*). That is, neither the empirical nor the existential-ontological elements of a truth claim can exist alone. They are *aspects* of the same truth claim and not independant elements of it. Every "empirical" claim is couched in language which inescapably refers to ideal essences of which this or that experience are *types*. Even a radically new experience would be new only by comparison with types of experience that are familiar. And every delineation of a phenomenological essence or of an "existential" presupposes not just the perceptual givenness of the essence (as in Merleau-Ponty) but a *commitment* to it as a given *reality* in which we live and carry on the ordinary business of the day: the empirical reality to which we refer when we speak of our understanding of how things *are* in the world.

While these two aspects of any knowledge-claim cannot be separated from each other in any radical way, they do seem, however, to be different enough from each other to permit a certain amount of relatively independent insight in each aspect. The reference back to the other aspect, however, is more immediate, stronger, and more urgent in the interests of truth in the case of inner, tensional cross-referencing than in the case of cross-referencing *between* domains. A truth-claim in any one domain is most significant when some kind of balance, effected by a consistent, coherent, mutual reference of both aspects, is manifested in the truth-claim. Thus, cross-referencing of a special kind goes on *within* each domain of knowledge: it is a cross-referencing which operates under the *tension* of two *polar* aspects of any domain of knowledge, a tension which makes the mutual correction or confirmation function much more immediately within the organic whole of the domain.

This type of mutually corrective or confirming cross-referencing contrasts with the type that goes on *between* domains. As we shall see, this latter type of cross-referencing is much more free and lacks the tension of the former type. The tensions that exist between truth claims of different domains are generated in different degrees by the nature of the relation of the domains themselves. Sharply contrasting truth claims brought to loggerheads in two different domains can generate considerable tension, which is quite effective in producing much cross-referencing activity. But the tension is never the same as the *natural* tension of aspects *within* a domain: it must be generated by the active choice which brings different domains together in one focus, and it may not demand resolution quite as strongly in order for one domain or the other to make some sort of coherent knowledge-claim. The interplay between domains is much more *free* and, when correction of confirmation occurs, the effects are understood in more than one domain of knowledge. This second type of cross-referencing activity I have opted to designate "free, interplaying cross-referencing" between domains. Thus, I have distinguished two types of mutually corrective or confirming cross-referencing activity: the inner, tensional type, which goes on *within* domains, and the *free, interplaying* type, which goes on *between* or *among* domains.

How shall we decide which ideas from one domain are too foreign to be acceptable within another, even through some sort of synthesis? Or, on the other hand, how shall we determine that they properly act to discredit ideas in another domain? Much needs to be done in the development of criteria here, as well as in the analysis of the whole dynamic of cross-referencing. But we can begin to generate some dynamic activity in this process if we simply adopt Macquarrie's own notion that ideas which are broadly "reasonable" in a "loose" rational sense are acceptable, no matter in what domain they may occur. Thus, we can reject outright any ideas that are self-contradictory or any proposals that contradict *in strictly logical terms* other ideas that are held to be true. This does not exclude the formation of paradoxes or an assertion of mystery, which do not rely for their character on logical contradiction or self-referential inconsistency. Ideas that are "foreign" to a particular domain (e.g., ethical ideas of right and wrong considered within a domain governed by aesthetic criteria) may emerge as supportive or "neutral" or disconfirming of ideas in *either* or *both* domains. And as they do so, either a new synthesis emerges or else disconfirmation and retreat generally occurs. If a neutral function is maintained, the cross-referencing activity can either go to other ideas within the cross-referencing domains as well as to those of other domains to seek ways of effecting synthesis or disconfirmation, or else it can remain "incomplete". "Completion" might be understood as a "resting place" in the dynamic, constituted by the emergence of a new synthesis which must be explored, analyzed, and "profundized", or else by a retreat and regrouping of ideas within one or both domains (and possibly others which have been connected to the particular cross-referencing in question). The cross-referencing dynamic is never really completed and occurs among all domains at all times. It counts as "worthless speculation" only those ideas which are proposed in such a way as to make their engagement in the cross-referencing dynamic virtually impossible or in principle unfruitful. But many ideas which one domain or another might count as speculation, if they can be made to enter into the cross-referencing dynamic in a way that promises results, can be accepted as functional commitments (i.e., as ideas to which we can to some degree commit ourselves in order to generate a promising cross-referencing activity; we must remember that the energy for the cross-referencing dynamic comes from the conflict or support of ideas to which we are to some degree committed. For only in this way can an emergent synthesis be also a higher unity of being). When the dynamic has bogged down or stagnated, a "speculative" idea can regenerate motion, which is fruitful even if it only serves to discredit finally the speculative idea. Thus, cross-referencing opens up the *whole* dynamic of coming to truth as an adventure of the mind and soul. No one tyrannical criterion for truth can *a priori* reduce our grasp of truth to one particular form and exclude other refereshing inroads to higher truth. Apart from logical contradiction, all *a priori* reductionism must give way to this broadly empirical and phenomenological methodology.

We can illustrate the inner, tensional dynamic of cross-referencing in a general way by examining briefly the domains of science, history, and religion (or theology). These have been domains to which Macquarrie has constantly referred throughout his works and which are interdependently powerful in forming his total view of truth about the nature of God, man, and reality. We will consider first each of these domains in relation to phenomenological-existential knowledge.

Each domain establishes itself by a "break" that occurs in the phenomenological-existential interconnections of ideas when we try to reverse the alethic process and deduce concrete events. Science is a broad, general type of knowledge which forms a domain organized around broad interdependent categories such as sense experience, cause, explanation, falsifiability, etc. The *contingency* of experience and knowledge is most pronounced in the scientific domain. The *factual* nature of knowledge arises here as a description of what actually, concretely, takes place in the world; and the facts are organized in a way in which one contributes to an explanation of the other, generally by reference to the causes for their contingent being. Centering around sense experience, contingency, and causal explanation, the scientific domain is the most obviously empirical of all domains.

We have noted that Macquarrie has an ambiguous relationship to whatever we might call facts. He is ready enough to deal with the scientific, factual domain as a phenomenologist (Indeed, his notion of a hierarchical ordering of beings is grounded in his phenomenological ontology of nature as revealed in the sciences; and this notion, which involves the concept of synthesis of knowledge into higher, more unifying concepts as well as the achievement of new unities of *being*, has been applied both by him and by me to the fundamental dynamic of development in knowledge and being in other domains of knowledge. Further investigation would, no doubt, show that it is applicable in *all* domains of knowledge.). But Macquarrie has demonstrated an uneasiness with science as a domain of knowledge. He prefers to define truth as *aletheia* and to identify this with the disclosure of structures of being which can be described from various modes of experience. This definition leaves the notion of scientific truth, or empirical truth, unclarified.

The location of the "weight" of the concept of truth on the empirical side of the cross-referencing relation clarifies the concept of truth in the sciences without denying the validity of phenomenological truth. To be sure, the line of demarcation between the sciences and phenomenology is not absolutely clear, since much remains to be clarified, e.g., in the questions concerning what is "given" in sense data and concerning the nature of causal relations, among other important issues. But this clarity will never be gained without actively engaging in the mutually corrective and confirming cross-referencing which is essential to both aspects of scientific knowledge.

Empirical experience, taken in the broad sense of our experience of a natural world full of sights, sounds, tastes, etc., all of which show some degree of order and rhythm even in our most piquant experiences of chaos, is a "thereness" of experience which is spilling over with unclarified notions and meaning. It is never simply present as a comprehensible "unit" which needs no further questions and which raises no further issues. We *live* in it and, to a large degree, *by* the notions it seems to spawn. We come to a focus of experience relying and trusting tacitly on many elements of experience which go to constitute our more focussed engagements in empirical reality. We come to these engagements already to some degree *committed* and *dwelling by faith* in certain notions which we may have accepted only tacitly. This structure of tacit reliance for the sake of achieving certain foci may be extended all the way from fundamental perceptions and skills to conceptual knowledge.[2] Thus, any perception or concept is "spilling over" with the "promise" of discoveries yet to be made and knowledge yet to be clarified.

Part of this clarification and discovery process can be achieved only by a phenomenological-existential analysis of the knowing process as it occurs within the scientific domain. This analysis brings to the concrete experience a context of types and possibilities of experience—and, ultimately, of natural being—which unfolds its meaning by placing it "in context". The exercise of imagination in constructing varying possibilities and types on the basis of concrete experience yields ideas for empirical strategies of testing and clarifying certain ideas. The "promise" of concrete experience is fulfilled by the phenomenological clarification which "extends" the concepts and notions generated by the experience to concepts which may well aid in establishing causal explanations and other empirical relations. The insight that certain mental illnesses are instances of biological disease rather than perversions of the soul, e.g., has much to do with establishing cause and effect relationships and recommending treatment programs.

The phenomenological-existential aspect of scientific truth grows and develops along with the empirical aspect. An exploration in the empirical realm yields a concrete discovery which is also a yet to be explicitated phenomenological type or possibility which has not been integrated into the existential-ontological system. Some discoveries might demand a re-modification of this aspect of scientific truth by disconfirming that a certain kind of concrete being or, dynamic within natural being belongs to the type indicated in phenomenological-existential analysis. Cross-referencing may yield confirmations, disconfirmation, retreats, and developments from either aspect of scientific truth, all of which contribute ultimately to the emergence of new syntheses. These syntheses never constitute any final monolithic integration of the two aspects of scientific truth but rather point always to yet unexplored territory which we approach from new perspectives and, possibly as well, to new unities of being.

The fundamental relationship between the two "inner, tensional" cross-referencing aspects of truth in the scientific domain, then, consists in this: imaginative and adventurous phenomenological-existential investigations can "fill out" the meanings of scientific discoveries and point in the direction of new discoveries and fuller explanations; and a similar exploration of what is revealed in empirical data, especially concerning how empirical realities do in fact "hang together", can clarify and correct existential-ontological knowledge. "Synthesis" is conceptual and ontological for the knowing agent.

A similar inner, tensional cross-referencing activity occurs in historical knowledge, which is more intimately connected with the sciences than other domains. History focuses on the past; it tries to establish what actually happened, couching its language to a large degree in descriptions and explanations that refer to empirical and sensible experience. Thus, its truth is constituted by stories (not simply propositions) which describe as accurately as possible, with all necessary explanations given, what happened in the empirical sense in the occurrence of particular events.

The historical realm of knowledge does not have its own "break" with a system of existential-ontological structures. It *presupposes* the break of contingency which the sciences effect in establishing themselves as a domain in their own right. Perhaps this is the reason why some historians and philosophers have attempted to make this domain somehow subservient to the sciences. For it stresses the empirical aspect of truth which it holds, except for its interest in the past, in common with the sciences. Indeed, just as in the sciences, one cannot reason from existential-ontological knowledge to a knowledge of the contingent events which, in the case of history, occurred in the past. History is *contingent*. Events have simply happened without any obvious ultimate "reason".

Even if we cannot at this time settle the issues relating to historical study, such as the notion of the past, the question whether it is a science or whether "laws" can be discerned it it, and the question of whether a phenomenology of history is possible, we can discern that both phenomenological-existential and empirical knowledge are active in historical knowledge. Existential-ontological knowledge unfolds the meaning of historical events by extending the concept of what *did* happen, through imaginative variation, etc., into general structures which define types of historical events (e.g., war, depression, radical change, fixed stability, etc.). These general structures "fill out" unlived historical possibilities in imaginative constructions of "intuited, valid interconnections of types of events", which enrich our knowledge of the historical domain immediately by pointing to things that *might* have happened but *did* not. Further, these structures, applied to the empirical study of history, can point our gaze in directions which are only possibilities from where we stand but which advances concrete historical knowledge whenever an exploration based on the possibilities they disclose leads to a hitherto undiscovered aspect of concrete historical events.

The empirical study of history concerns itself with the *evidences* for an interpretation of past events and with techniques of investigation which seeks out evidence. And, as it engages in its task, it discovers the concrete facts of history which, in turn, "spill over" into the phenomenological disclosure of new types, possibilities, or simply providing the lived content of what would otherwise be formal essential types of events.

The inner, tensional cross-referencing relationship is, then, an active dynamic in the historical domain. This relationship between empirical history and existential-ontological knowledge is mutually correcting and confirming as well, since concrete historical facts may suggest new types of events or disconfirm that a particular event was of a suspected type. It might demonstrate that certain "types" of events cannot exist at all; or else it might discover that history occurred in a different way than previously understood, based on investigations suggested by the possibilities of events and their general structure disclosed in phenomenological-existential exploration.

The historical domain, then, is a broadly empirical mode of knowledge formed in mutually confirming and correcting cross-referencing relationship with the phenomenological-existential aspect of truth which merges into the general ontological and symbolic knowledge of reality grasped from the historical perspective. The energy for the cross-referencing dynamic is provided by our faith-commitments, our "indwelling", in regard to the truth we believe is at least partially established and which always touched on some degree of objective knowledge. As we perform the cross-referencing activity in pursuit of historical truth, we find new syntheses which restructure our understanding of history and open new pathways of being for us.

We may finally conclude this discussion of the cross-referencing aspects of truth within domains by showing how religion is involved in this same dynamic. Macquarrie tends to identify the higher, analogical language about Being with language about God.[3] Indeed, he seems to want to enter into the domain of theology by a translation, which he understands as an act of faith, of analogical language about Being into language about God. We can, however, avoid the problems inherent in this surreptitious identity of ontology and theology by viewing religion as a domain of truth in its own right which shares the cross-referencing relationship that all other domains possess. For certainly the existential-ontological structures that are disclosed in the alethic dimension of truth do not entail the contingent experience of the *mysterium tremendum et fascinans* and the dimension of awareness of Being which we as Christians can then only call God because of the personal encounter we grasp through this experience. The *mysterium tremendum* is not identical with a systematic alethic aspect of truth in the religious domain. It represents the "break" which we can but do not necessarily experience upon reversing the uni-directional unfolding of the meaning of the religious domain of experience and knowledge. When it occurs, it clearly establishes this domain as a domain in its own right.

But this is not the only source of the break that makes religion a domain of experience and knowledge in its own right. *Faith* is an act of the person in which he chooses to *indwell* his total understanding of things as touching somehow on the reality of a personal God (at least in a culture which predisposes one to Judaism or Christianity). This faith engenders a certain way of experiencing things and may issue in the *mysterium* experience. Faith understands these experiences as grounded in a transcendent reality which relates to man of its own initiation in terms of grace, providence, atonement, and the self-communication of a personal God which touches and transforms one's own concrete reality. Faith is an indwelling in a "final" or "ultimate" interpretation of our "feeling" for Mystery in its concrete and personal encounter and the *Mysterium* that grounds it. It understands reality in essentially *religious* terms, which for the Christian are quite different from a grasp of an ontology which lends its support to this understanding. The religious understanding cannot be reduced to ontology nor consist of a *mere* interpretation of it in its own terms. It is grounded in an empirical encounter with a transcendent reality which somehow presses itself in on man's situation in existence and is experienced in unexpected and concrete ways. Thus, Christians distinguish between "knowing the Lord" and having a knowledge of ontology or even the more impersonal and purely intellectual elements of theology.

The ontology which Macquarrie wishes to identify by translation of faith as religious language is, then, to be viewed as developed partially out of the cross-referencing relationship established within the religious domain by the concrete encounter of a transcendent reality which somehow touches us personally and as personal. It consists, within the religious domain, in a grasp of the *meaning* of these experiences and the structures of Being they imply or suggest, disclosed through phenomenology and existential analytic. It grows out of the empirical encounter and is enhanced, confirmed, and corrected by the assertion of the lived experience which interprets itself in the context of phenomenological-existential analysis. This analysis establishes types of religious experiences and possibilities of religious existence, thus "situating" our particular, concrete experiences in a wider scope of possibilities and clarifying their nature as well as pointing toward the meaning they have as part of an essential structure. But this structure, this analysis, is never complete. It relies on the concrete experiences it analyzes, and this experience "spills over" the meanings garnered by it and generates the continued search for a more adequate ontological grasp. Indeed, the empirical aspect of the religious domain of knowledge may provide data that can radically change our understanding of Being. Of course, the reverse may happen as well: our grasp of Being that flows out of religious experience may direct our intentional gaze toward new hitherto hidden areas of experience within the religious domain which engender in turn transformation of the religious understanding. The cross-referencing relationship is functional within the domain of religious knowledge, then, as in all other domains.

The concrete, experiential aspect of the religious domain is preserved in this description and seems to be true to the experience of Christians throughout the history of the church. Christians have been most dynamic in their faith when they have believed deeply that God was touching their concrete lives.

His reality has been often concieved by Christians almost wholly in these terms rather than in philosophical or ontological ones. Within Christian faith, personal regeneration, grace, supernatural peace and capacity to love, *et alia*, are not merely personal readjustments to the demands of life in view of a deepened ontological understanding of things but are involved with concrete phenomena that impinge on our lives from a reality we perceive as transcendent; and our knowledge of this *source* of life for us is incomplete without an attempt to understand it as one understands a person in his concrete reality as well as in his deeper, ontological dimensions. Our empirical assertions must be judged first within the context of faith itself; and this context loses its vitality, richness, and *truth* when it is understood merely as a grasp of the Being which we view impersonally as a "structure".

We may now turn to the "second" level of the cross-referencing relationship that we have thus far described only as occurring *within* each domain. This second level consists in the cross-referencing relationship that occurs *between* two or more different domains of knowledge, the free, interplaying level. Indeed, all domains of knowledge have some degree of interdependence and all engage together, continuously and contemporaneously, in the interplay of cross-referencing. We will examine only the ways in which the domain of religious knowledge interrelates to the other domains we have thus far given brief analysis, and we will not even attempt to describe their contemporaneous interrelations together with the religious domain. But the following analysis will be adequate to illustrate the basic principles of free interplay.

Before entering directly into the analysis of free interplay, however, we should pause, by way of developing further the concept of the interplay of domains, to note the role that language plays in this process.

The establishment of interdependent and interplaying domains of knowledge, all of which are undergirded by the existential-ontological knowledge and regional phenomenologies that profundize their meaning and enrich and enhance their discoveries and interplaying syntheses, produces a kind of reasoning and thinking that is governed by rules and criteria unique for each domain. That is the defining characteristic of the "domain".

This implies that a specialized vocabulary, particular rules of usage or "grammar", etc., in the language which speaks within a particular domain will differ in various ways from that of other domains. This corresponds to what Macquarrie, with Wittgenstein, calls "language-games". Language-games are not self-subsistent games, as Wittgenstein seemed to think and for which Macquarrie criticizes him. They are "families" of games with kinship to forms of language in other games, though each family member remains somehow unique. The use of language obeys rules within the domain, but a surplus of meaning within the rules of usage and the kinship of use of important terms in each language-game manifests as an imaginative play of meaning which corresponds to two fundamental synthesizing acts: (1) the interplay between phenomenological knowledge and the empirical experience of the domain itself and (2) the interplay among domains themselves.

The question concerning how to "speak" of the fundamental reality to which language refers is not resolved by pointing to a "hidden assumption of Being" in language or by resting in the rules of ordinary language. *All* knowledge involves a faith-commitment in which one indwells the structures of the various domains of knowledge, investing their criteria with the power to judge the fruitfulness of the ideas generated within it through a process of discovery and free imaginative play. We must be sensitive to the marks of truth within each domain. We can always say that *something* of reality is known, even if that something is given shape and content by an act of faith which is open to its own discrediting and which accepts as true only ideas that are clearly indicated (if not empirically established or implied) by each domain's criteria. Ideas that are not contradictory to truths in any other domain and are consonant with all can be speculative adventures *worth taking* and as such must be given a serious place as an exploration of undisclosed areas of knowledge.

With this understanding of language firmly in mind, we can follow Macquarrie in avoiding many philosophical errors by giving up our natural predisposition to believe that language is supposed to say things "perfectly clearly" and in a manner which can be technically expanded toward a true, "scientific" grasp of things. Language functions as a tool to lead us to truth within a domain or as a synthesis between or among domains, i.e., to higher syntheses and new unities of being. It opens us up to reality and is the place where reality is disclosed most profoundly. We can now turn to the notion of the interplay of domains, which requires an adoptive and flexible structure of language.

Notes

1. Wolfhart Pannenburg, Jesus, *God and Man* (London, 1968), pp. 74—88 and 88—106.
   Panneburg's own view of the nature of historical facts is quite different from mine, since he does not explicitly integrate the methods of existential and phenomenological analysis into his work in the manner in which I have done in this work. Furthermore, he does not explicitly develop a theory of domains of knowledge in the manner in which I have done here. But his notion of an historical fact is compatible with mine, especially in so far as he sees concrete facts as established not merely within the domain of a historical methodology itself but as a kind of interplay between such methodology and other aspects of thought. Thus, we find him asserting, "Intuition does not open an 'immediate, prescientific relationship to past history, across centuries and millenia, *which bears within itself unconditional certainty about this past life* . . .' ". (p. 99) And this statement, which asserts the

weakness of a purely historical approach, can be placed together with the following one, which defines an historical fact in terms of the recognition of an eschatalogical hope which functioned in the first Christian community: "Thus the resurrection of Jesus would be designated as a historical even in this sense: If the emergence of primitive Christianity, which, apart from other traditions, is also traced back by Paul to appearances of the resurrected Jesus, can be understood in spite of all critical examination of the tradition only if one examines it in the light of the eschatological hope for a resurrection from the dead, then that which is so designated is a historical event, even if we do not know anything more particular about it." (p. 98).

2. Cf., Michael Polanyi, *The Tacit Dimension* (Garden City, N.Y., 1967), pp. 1—25. Macquarrie uses these terms in the development of his epistemology under the influence of Polanyi.
3. We should note that some modification of this view is to be found in his most recent work, *In Search of Deity: An Essay in Dialectical Theism* (London, 1984), cf. pp. 173—184. Here Macquarrie presents a dialectical concept of God in which symbol certainly functions, but it seems to function in a more rational context, since it grows out of mutually necessary but conflicting conceptual notions of aspects of the Deity. The mystic may have the right to use metaphor and symbol more freely (cf., pp. 185—198); but the theologian and philosopher ought to rely on a more carefully developed rational progression in conceiving God, a progression grounded in a dialectial interplay between conflicting ideas. This development in Macquarrie's theology tends to confirm the wider project I have proposed in making each domain of knowledge part of the interplay he proposes. My proposal is a much wider one, though it is very much in consonance with Macquarrie's more restricted concept of interplay. I would reject the term "dialectical" as a defining characteristic of the interplay of domains (though something very much like dialectical interplay does indeed at times occur), because the word "dialectic" generally implies "opposition" between terms, and I think interplay, while it demands "difference" between ideas, does not require opposition, much less an oppositional *dyad* of terms.

Final words: The Interplay of Domains

We have seen that each domain is constituted in its own right by means of a "break" in the phenomenologically unified structure of Being that is effected when we reverse the uni-directional unfoldment of meaning and turn back again to the experiences upon which they are grounded. This break involves an "empirical" element in the domainic structure which is established according to a "broad" empiricism which Macquarrie recommends. Each domain is developed and enriched by an "inner, tensional" mutually corrective cross-referencing between the broadly empirical and more proximate and concretely real grasp of the experience upon which the break is founded and the wider description of the structures of being which are disclosed by a phenomenological-existential analysis of this experience. Each domain is "profundized" by the resulting intellectual syntheses that emerge from this interplay. Each synthesis represents a grasp of a higher unity of Being, which is defined according to the content and form given by these higher syntheses, the "surplus" of meaning sensed in both experience, and the analysis that unfolds it, which "burgeons" with new yet hidden syntheses and "promises" them.

This promise is fulfilled only in the context of an even more intricate relationship between domains, involving the interrelationship of truth-claims of entire domains themselves. For domains of knowledge never exist and develop in isolation but are interconnected with one another in the context of a language which speaks of them as "family members" rather than as isolated kingdoms. Science, e.g., has developed to some degree in partnership with religion, even if they have often been at odds. History and science share an intimate relation in terms of methodology and empirical grounding. Religion and history have often been in mutually confirming relationship, and ethics and religion have especially been so.

The interrelationship of all domains of knowledge is far too broad and complex even to be described here, to say nothing of receiving a detailed analysis. It would include many other domains than I have thus far mentioned and all of their synthetic profundizing in relationship to existential-ontological analysis. That is the subject matter of a whole, systematic approach to philosophy, which I am recommending as the best procedure for unfolding the promise in each domain. All I wish to do is recommend the cross-referencing methodology, which I feel is consonant with the general thrust of Macquarrie's philosophy and theology, and to suggest some ways of viewing this complex interrelationship in relation only to the domain of religion.

We have already described at least the key ideas in the relationship between religion and its profundizing syntheses through inner, tensional mutually corrective cross-referencing between its concrete, empirical aspect and existential and phenomenological analysis. As we enter into the relationships which obtain between religion and other domains of knowledge, the concept of mutual correction, which is explicitly stated as part of the cross-referencing approach I recommend, becomes more visibly functional. For, when we enter into the religious domain itself and view from there the claims of other domains, the contours of conflict and sympathy with them become more visible. Claims which we make as theologians may conflict with or confirm claims made by science, history and other domains. And this means that our commitments, our indwelling of a comprehension within any domain, are often threatened or supported, depending on the nature of the relationship one domain has to another.

We cannot rest content either with conflict *or* support. If there is conflict, we sense division with the very center of our being, which naturally tends to wholeness and seeks higher unities of personal wholeness (only a discussion of the ethical domain can clarify this statement, a discussion I intend for another work). If we find support, the same tendency urges us to push forward into the higher syntheses that are promised there and seek a completion that is always on the way, if it is never fully achieved. The complex interrelationship of domains is burgeoning with the promise of higher syntheses to be born our of the conflict *and* support that they lend each other.

We can go back to Macquarrie's "loose" empirical criterion for what is an "acceptable" or "rational" idea in any domain: Whatever is not either self-contradictory or contradictory to other deeply believed ideas and is in some kind of consonance with what is believed elsewhere is an "acceptable" idea. This loose criterion for the acceptability of an idea in one domain by the general structure of another seems to open up the fields of philosophy and theology to an adventurous and stimulating way of emerging into higher syntheses of knowledge and being.

We can illustrate this by reference to the religious domain. In the case of the relationship between religion and history, for example, we can enter into a procedure of mutually corrective cross-referencing that can open new doors to knowledge in both domains. The claim made by theologians, e.g., that Jesus Christ was resurrected from the dead does not have to be viewed as *merely* a different "kind" of claim from those made by historians. This is generally done in order to avoid the sense of conflict that arises around this claim as issued by theologians and denied by most historians. It certainly does function in religion in ways that differ from and far exceed the function it would have if it were claimed by historians. But theologians often believe, and most Christians in company with Macquarrie believe, that unless this claim *also* has a strictly historical meaning, its other functions in religion are discredited or greatly weakened to a point of encompassing only the psychological effects of belief. The conflict generated demands a response which is not adequately represented by *reducing* resolving historical claims to the existential transformations exercised by faith.

Macquarrie, as we have seen, equivocates on just this issue, being caught between an insight that the historical claim must be maintained (which he believes Bultmann also has) and a commitment to follow a Bultmannian line of interpretation in which this insight gets lost and virtually denied in his relegation of such historical claims to ''speculation''.

But he need not end up in this position. For his philosophy and theology provide means to deal with this dilemma. If historical evidences can go only so far, and if theological claims cannot in themselves offer rational proofs of historical events, we can still make these claims as theologians whenever they do not logically contradict deep beliefs held in other domains and are not self-contradictory or otherwise obviously absurd and if they are consonant with other important and widely believed ideas. The loose, empirical criterion of rationality which Macquarrie recommends is very useful in bridging the two conflicting domains. Whatever is self-contradictory or contradictory in the strict, logical sense or else is simply not ''consonant'' with the evidences in each conflicting domain is unacceptable. If either history or religion makes such claims, then one domain can act to correct the other by referencing the idea across the two domains to examine its evidences and its ''fit''. If the idea is ''consonant'', then it can be believed. But all beliefs are, in effect, faith-indwellings which eventually reveal their fruitfulness for emergence or their inadequacy. An idea that proves itself inadequate in *either* domain can be finally rejected by *both*. An idea that proves itself adequate in one domain but is ''neutral'' or indifferent to the criteria of the other is acceptable as an exploratory idea in the other. An idea that is neutral in both can be accepted in both as an exploratory idea, but has value mostly when there is stagnation in the domains concerned and some avenue to discovery is needed. Pursuing truth by integrating such ideas is a risk of faith but is justified speculation. Such speculation is unjustified, however, when alternative pathways to discovery exist and certainly when the failure to follow them is grounded in prejudice.

Religion and history, then, stand in a dynamic relationship of mutually corrective cross-referencing activity. In conjunction with other domains as well, they seek to fulfill the incompleteness that is part of every domain by a continuous, interdependent growth and mutually assisted modification toward the emergence of new syntheses that represent new discoveries and new unities of being. More concretely, a theological conviction that demonstrates adequacy in the religious domain, that leads fruitfully to promised discoveries in the domain itself and is easily profundized in existential knowledge, might be applied, if it is consonant, to the historical realm and lead to a discovery in historical methodology or fact which makes a higher synthesis of ideas between religion and history possible. And this synthesis itself, when developed further in existential analysis, may lead to the emergence of a yet higher level of understanding. In reference to the resurrection, e.g., the evidences seem to be such that it is an adequate idea in the theological realm but only a consonant one (at best, and in a purely logical sense) in the historical realm, at least as Christians have portrayed the evidences. But we may, through confessing the resurrection as Christians—and this means confessing belief in its objective reality as historians—seek to understand what the resurrection means in the historical domain as well as in other domains. We may press forward our conviction until, perhaps by the grace of God, we emerge into a higher synthesis of understanding in which the resurrection finds further historical confirmation. We may never accomplish this confirmation, but the movement toward it is not simply speculation as Macquarrie says it is; it is the activity of a faith properly seeking understanding. We may not know that such activity *will* have a definite outcome; but our engagement in it is justified as part of a process of emergence that is our natural right. And we must be prepared as well, when we engage in this process, to discover historical truths which disconfirm the idea and undercut the power of the truth in religion as well. For if we take Macquarrie's remarks on Karl Popper seriously, any attempt to test the adequacy of an idea or claim within another domain (i.e., one other than its own), must be able to accept a claim of falsification. In Macquarrie's terms, "falsification" means that the idea is inadequate; and I interpret this to mean, on the level of domain knowledge, that it does not fulfil any promise of emergence.

Finally, the most commonly noted relationship between two recognized domains is that between science and religion. Much has been written about the relationship between these two domains, and I don't intend to raise and solve all of the pertinent issues concerning their relationship in this work. But I will simply note that the same mutually corrective dynamic of cross-referencing is active here and has many historical illustrations of higher syntheses. If I may be allowed the unjustified assertion that evolution is basically true, I can point to the synthesis of this idea with the concept of creation as an excellent example. Originally, the concept of evolution was thought to be utterly opposed to the claims of Christian theology. Presupposing a mechanical necessity which functioned through eternal cosmic space and time, the notion of evolution contrasted sharply with a literally interpreted Biblical notion of creation by a personal, willing God. But neither idea was contradictory in the other domain (Deism had prepared the way for an evolutionary idea in theology as well as a creationist possibility in the sciences); and, given the necessity of finding some solution to the conflict that these two contrasting but consonant ideas generated, a synthesis was finally grasped and made simple for the everyday, believing, but scientifically aware, Christian. Science tells us *how* God created the word, while theology assures us *that* he created it. God and science were no longer bitter enemies, and the higher synthesis, which consists in a modified notion of creation, has been fruitful in developing the notion of God as well as deepening our view of the world as science views it.

Science and religion, of course, have many other points of mutual correction and confirmation. Religion was corrected and had to retreat from the earlier synthesis it had effected with the Aristotelian cosmology under the auspices of Thomistic theology when science finally forced its collapse with the work of Galileo and Copernicus. Science had to retreat, on the other hand, from cosmologies and unproved philosophical points of view such as impersonal and rigid cosmic determinism when theological thought, in concert with philosophical analysis, showed them to be untenable as held and offered reasonable alternatives, such as "proofs" of God's existence. More recent scientific assertions, such as the Heisenburg uncertainty principle and the equation of matter and energy in atomic physics, have tended to produce some confirming ideas for the religious domain. And teleological proofs for God's existence depended heavily on scientific thought, especially that drawn from biology.

The dynamic we have already outlined in the relationship religion has with history is, perhaps, more visible in its relationship with the sciences. Higher syntheses are produced and indwelt with consequences of profundization under phenomenological-existential analysis; and fruitful growth is produced in both domains because of it. Correction and retreat occurs in both domains, with consequences of a loss of unity. As a core of truth steadily grows, man has emerged into higher unities of understanding, informed by the syntheses and discoveries generated out of this relationship. He has, e.g., emerged from the superstition and frightful fantasy that hovered over medieval "science" and religion to face God as a human being loved in grace in a world created and intended as good.

We must remember, of course, that religion does not have isolated one-to-one relationships with each different domain. It is carrying on the relationship of mutually correcting and confirming cross-referencing with *all* the different domains at once. And these include far more than the handful we have explicitly related to religion. Further, these are *all* carrying on the same relationship with *each other*. Many small corrections, confirmations, syntheses, dissolutions, etc., are constantly taking place, and often wide-ranging, important ones are in question. The task of theology lies in fulfilling the natural drive for wholeness, which is the impetus toward truth in *each* domain, by contributing to the emergence into higher levels of being through the syntheses it can effect. Theology is not the queen of the sciences; it is one domain among others. But it is, for the Christian, an irreducible dimension of the religious domain even if it must cooperate with the other domains if we are to find higher syntheses in any domain. Wherever religion has stagnated, all being has stagnated (E.g., Egypt's 4000 years of "stability" in pre-Christian times). *Each* domain bears a responsibility to the whole project of higher emergence, which is the natural direction of the completion of man, as experienced in different forms in each domain.

I cannot begin to outline the complexities of this task. I can only suggest that viewing the future of theology as an essential element in this difficult and wide-ranging task is a necessary propadeutic to entering with the spirit of adventure and faith into new insights into Being and God. And perhaps the higher syntheses, emergent levels which grow out of such a task, will lead us to new worlds of truth and a new relationship between God and man.

I think this view of theology, though it sounds quite different from the theology of Macquarrie, is really only an implication of what he really intends for theology. It preserves a phenomenological base and the validity of existential analysis, though it avoids seeing degrees of truth as an adequacy defined solely by this sort of knowledge. Existential-ontological knowledge deepens the truth grasped in a particular domain by relating it to the notion of Being and describing how the truth in a domain manifests something of a wider structure of Being. But this is not the sole meaning which I have applied to the notion of adequacy. For I think relating this notion to the empirical and concrete truths which are claimed *within* domains functions to resolve the ambiguity Macquarrie manifests when he speaks of truth in any domain. I have adopted his concept of domains and made it a key element in my attempt to show a way in which Macquarrie's theology can unfold in a direction of which I think he can approve without sacrificing too much of what he affirms in a sometimes inconsistent way. Thus, I have preserved his commitment to maintaining the objectivity of history and preserved a means (existential analysis) by which its *meaning* is made miscible with it while avoiding a collapse into Bultmannian hermeneutic. I have picked up his affirmation of a "broad" empiricism, molded it to his agreement with Popper's falsifiability criterion, and integrated it with his commitment to existential phenomenology to preserve a means of speaking of different kinds of knowledge in different domains, all of which somehow impinge on a single project of finding the truth of Being. I have employed his philosophy of language to undergird this pluralization of domains and have, with all of this, resolved many of his ambiguities concerning the nature of truth and Being. I have, finally, made religion a domain among others, not to be identified with the general pursuit of emergence to higher levels of understanding. And this has clarified the "relationship" he has implied between these two domains of truth (the religious and the philosophical) while avoiding a confused identity of them.

I cannot say in the end whether Macquarrie would approve my interpretation of him and my re-arrangement of his ideas. I think what I have suggested here presents a way out of most of his difficulties and that it preserves much of his philosophy and theology while being true to what he *intends* for truth in the religious domain.

It seems appropriate to end this work with a comment on his most recent work, *In Search of Deity*. For Macquarrie begins in this work to break away from a more purely existential ground for theology in favor of a wider approach which utilizes more freely the methodology of empirical thinkers as well as that of thinkers more committed to an exploration of categories by means of rational thought. I believe that in this work Macquarrie begins to develop toward a pluralization of domains of knowledge in which the various domains are developed by means of some sort of interplay between them. Macquarrie calls this interplay a "dialectical" one, grounded in an opposition of ideas. He asserts that various opposing ideas about God can be "thought through" by means of a dialectical interplay, so that a third, "synthesizing" idea can emerge which maintains what is of value in each opposing idea while "breaking through" to a new, more profound idea. Certainly my own proposal is consonant with this development in his theology, though my project forms a much wider context for theology and does not restrict itself to dialectical oppositions, though it legitimately includes them. Further, Macquarrie does not clearly distinguish, as I have, between the interplay between aspects of knowledge within each domain (the empirical side of experience and the rational side of theory formation and conceptual structuralization which phenomenology provides) and the interplay which occurs between and among domains. My proposal provides a much more complex context for the development of knowledge in any domain, whereas Macquarrie's restriction to the dialectical mode in producing emergent ideas, while perhaps logically clearer, narrows the scope of interplay and reduces the free space for the development of ideas in any domain.

We can best understand this development in Macquarrie's theology by noting some of the statements he makes in his most recent book *In Search of Deity*. Noting that tensions arise between the "God of religion" and the "God of philosophy", Macquarrie, who already understands this tension basically in terms of a tension between experiential modes of knowing and rational modes of knowing (which I have described in terms of two interplaying aspects of knowledge within any domain of knowledge), proposes that we deal with such tensions by looking for "a more dialectical concept".[1] He says,

> These oppositions are not destructive contradictions or even sheer paradoxes of the "take it or leave it" variety. So far as possible, I must show that in every opposi-

tion, each side has its right and each side can and must be asserted. But I draw attention to the modifying expression, "so far as possible", for there must be limitations to any finite being's understanding of God. A "God" understood and neatly packaged in philosophical concepts would not be God.

This statement represents a clear re-evaluation of the program of existential theology, though it is as yet too undeveloped to make much of a difference in a total evaluation of Macquarrie's work. He explicitly states, however, that he is moving away from his previously higher estimation of certain aspects of Thomistic theology in affirming that Eriugena's name for God, "He who is more than being", is more subtle than Aquinas' "He who is".[2]

Macquarrie understands this definition of God as requiring, for its unfoldment, a dialectical approach in which both the empirical and rational aspects of knowledge are operative. And here he comes close to my own proposal of interplaying aspects of knowledge within domains. Thus, he says,

> God precedes all existences by being the condition of their existence, so he is not himself numbered almong the existents. That is part of the reason for the elusiveness of God, and explains why any empiricist philosophy, if it remains strictly empirical, has no place for God. Existence, as we understand it in our everyday dealings or as it is defined by empiricism, excludes God. Inevitably, he is nothing.[3]

Macquarrie then goes on to analyze a number of important dialectically opposed ideas which compose our concept of God: Existence-nothing, one-many, knowability-incomprehensibility, transcendence-imminence, passibility-impassibility, and eternity-temporality. The dialectial interplay between these notions (but not *among* the dialectically opposed pairs) produced notions of God which cannot be categorized by one-word definitions, but our understanding emerges into a more profound grasp of God than either of the opposed sides of a dialectical pair can offer.

This dialectical procedure, however, is firmly grounded in the empirical aspect of knowing God, which Macquarrie gives its rightful due under the rubric of "spirituality". He says,

> There is also a direct personal way of knowing, typified most clearly by the knowledge that one person has of another, but with many other forms besides, such as the knowledge one may have of a tract of countryside over which one has often walked, or the knowledge of some great musical work to which one has listened often. This kind of knowledge is not easily put into propositional form and cannot constitute a logical system. It is different from knowledge of facts, but it cannot be denied that it is genuine knowledge, and knowledge of a very important kind . . .
> The difference between theology and philosophy on the one hand and spirituality on the other is not that the former is cognitive and the latter is non-cognitive, but that both are cognitive in different ways. Theology and philosophy are successful to the extent that they find appropriate words in which to frame their knowledge

of God. Spirituality, on the other hand, seems to reach its peak when it leaves words behind and enters into a fulfilled silence. But can there be cognition or any form of knowledge without words? I think there can be. Michael Polanyi called it "tacit knowledge", and gave many examples, such as the skill of the builder or the skill of the research scientist. To some extent, these skills can be described and set out in books, but what is thus put into words is never exhaustive. There is something more that is unspecified and, however much we refine our language, unspecifiable.[4]

It is in this context in which Macquarrie identifies the mystic's grasp of God as somehow being "the last word" in Christian spirituality, a word which forms the highest peak of the experiential, concrete aspect of knowledge of God.

> There is a parallel here to the discernment of God . . . There is a vision (to use Whitehead's word) of a unity and wholeness pervading all things, and not a dead unity but one that pulsates with a life somehow akin to our own and which we call "spiritual".[5]

And he goes on to quote from the works of other theologians who are committed to an empirical ground in theology and whose works, he believes, are not incompatible with his own view of the empirical grounding of theology in a mystical experience which we all have to some degree. He carefully balances this aspect of knowing God with the need for theological reflection, however, showing that he clearly understands and forwards an interplay which at least occurs within the religious domain of knowledge:

> But spirituality needs theological reflection if it is not to run riot. On the other hand, theology and philosophy of religion become intolerably dry and lose all interest if we turn them into purely academic exercises and separate them from the life of the spirit.[6]

We must rejoice that the proposal I have made does find some confirmation in the recent developments of Macquarrie's philosophy and theology. Let us hope that this development will overcome its restriction to dialectical thought and broaden to grasp the interplay between domains of thought which will enrich theology endlessly.

Notes

1. John Macquarrie, *In Search of Deity: An Essay in Dialectical Theism.* (London, 1984), p. 171.
2. Ibid., p. 172.
3. Ibid., p. 173.
4. Ibid., pp. 188—189.
5. Ibid., p. 190.
6. Ibid., p. 193.

Appendix A: Bultmann

Macquarrie adopts a strong position on the limitations of demythologization, requiring an explicit response to the work of Bultmann. One finds scattered throughout his works a number of comments about Bultmann which, drawn together, make clear his critical stance in regard to him.

We may first note that Macquarrie appreciates the existential focus in Bultmann's theology:

> ... Bultmann relates both grace and revelation to a concrete event which for him is what he calls an "act of God", making its impact on human existence but originating beyond such existence. In so far as this act brings men to self-commitment and authentic life, it is experienced as grace; in so far as it brings them to a new self-understanding, it is experienced as revelation.[1]

Myth, then, according to Bultmann's existential interpretation, can be understood as contemporaneous with our present situation. This in itself is a fruitful focus for theology. Existential language, a language that describes self-understanding, could be stretched *via* an *analogia entis* to a language about Being. But Bultmann never works out this analogical language. He never moves from self-understanding to an understanding of Being.[2]

> The existentialists have tried to analyze the categories—or existentials—applicable to the being of man himself (*Existenz*). But that still leaves us without categories applicable to the ground of being, being itself beyond both *Vorhandenheit* and *Existenz*, that is to say, God. We can only speak of him by analogy or symbolically in categories drawn from *Vorhandenheit* or *Existenz*, as when we say that he is the first cause or that he is our Father in heaven. But already in the use of such symbols we are into the realm of the mythical.[3]

But the limitation of demythologization to a philosophy of self-understanding is not the only problem with Bultmann's work. Macquarrie claims that he is not consistent in the manner of applying the techniques of demythologization. If Bultmann wants to be consistent, he needs to extend demythologization to God's action in the world as well as to that of "demons". As it stands, however, he wants to say that God acts in the world and that this assertion is not mythology. Instead, it is a form of analogy which still somehow participates in a form of demythologization. But he does not distinguish the demything he effects through such analogical thinking from that which he employs on scripture.⁴ Hence, he ends up seeming to effect the same reductionism of theology to existential thought in the former which appears in the latter. Even if we note that his assertion of God is not too different from Heidegger's notion of a "call of conscience", which even Heidegger says *seems* to come from beyond us, we cannot avoid seeing Bultmann as an existential reductionist, however unintentional his final position might be. For, no matter how distant the call of conscience might seem to be, it does not, for either Heidegger or Bultmann, come from outside of us. It is the call of our own authentic existence.⁵

Further, Bultmann considers as myth both the gnostic dualism which Paul himself often demythologized and the objective-historical world in which Paul himself believed, the world of the first century. For this reason, the God of the New Testament, which Bultmann does not clearly distinguish from an understanding of God in general, can be spoken of only in mythical terms.⁶ God, then, is perceived only as being dramatically encountered at various times. Bultmann does not seem to admit a gradual development in our constant awareness of God. His understanding of God is individualistic and reliant wholly upon the Word, with no room left for a present encounter with him in, e.g., the sacraments. His failure to provide an ontological account of God, even by means of analogy, seems to be grounded in his unwillingness to objectify God, even though his theology would seem to demand such an ontological account. And this could be given without the objectification he wants to avoid.⁷ His God ends up being like the God of the Hebrew prophets, who disturbs us, shakes us out of complacency, drives us onward by His demand for justice and mercy, and confronts us in a way that shakes us out of ourselves.⁸ But such a notion of God, even if limited in its expression in scripture, is not consistent with Bultmann's assertion that the modern, average, quasi-scientific self-understanding should be *normative* in judging what is possible in Christian experience. This assertion may allow him to comfortably reject miracles, but it also rules out *a priori* any chance that God can reveal himself in the *kerygma* or act in history. And Bultmann does not want to deny that these are essential to any Christian theology.⁹

Bultmann, then, seems to be caught in a dilemma. If he exercises his program of demythologization with the full scope he intends, a scope which aims at translating all mythological language into worthwhile existential self-understanding, its consistent application makes it seemingly impossible to speak meaningfully about the subject of theology: God. And all language about God limits the scope of demythologization too tightly to make it a useful technique in New Testament interpretation. Macquarrie proposes to find a means wherein one can both gain an existential understanding of scripture (even a self-understanding mediated through scripture) and speak of God in terms which are neither mythical nor merely "existential". He believes that

Bultmann wanted to accomplish such a theology but fell into the traps formed by his inconsistent presuppositions. Thus, he proposes to succeed where Bultmann fails. Whether he succeeds in doing so is one of the issues of this book.

Notes

1. John Macquarrie, *The Scope of Demythologizing: Bultmann and his Critics* (London, 1960), p. 226.
2. John Macquarrie, *Principles of Christian Theology*, rev. ed. (London, 1977), pp. 133—134.
3. John Macquarrie, *An Existentialist Theology: A Comparison of Heidegger and Bultmann* (London, 1955), p. 174.
4. John Macquarrie, *God-Talk* (London, 1967), pp. 37—40.
5. *Loc. Cit.*
6. Macquarrie, *Existentialist Theology*, p. 174.
7. John Macquarrie, *Thinking About God* (London, 1975), pp. 188—189.
8. *Ibid.*, 187.
9. Macquarrie, *The Scope of Demythologizing*, pp. 235—237.

Appendix B: Demythologization

The scriptures are the major source for Christian faith and are the only source of our knowledge of the Jesus of history. Clearly, however, the world we live in today is not the same sort of world in which Christ lived and performed the deeds that are the subject of the *kerygma*. Our understanding of the nature of things, of human relations, of health and sickness, etc., are very much different from the understanding of such things in the time of Christ.

Macquarrie is not opposed to using the word "myth" to describe the Biblical events connected with Christ and the early church. For the gospel transcends particular verbal formulations. It has many dimensions (personal, social, imperative, interrogative, and descriptive) and cannot be fully expressed in any one situation or time.[1] It is essential that the gospel tell the story of Christ in terms which can only be described as "myth".

Macquarrie gives three fundamental definitions of myth, each of which seems to complement the others. First, he defines myth as an account which understands the divine in terms of human events.[2] He distinguishes here between myth and ideology, which he terms "quasi-myths".[3] Secondly, he defines a myth as a religious story that is *in principle* unverifiable and generally involves supernatural agents.[4] And third, he broadly defines mythology as the telling of imaginative stories, claiming that such stories are grounded in a genuine analogy between human experience of transcendence and the mysterious, transcendent universe. Myth is a creative, imaginative way of going beyond definition to an idea that can never be fully grasped.[5]

These definitions are actually ways of properly understanding myth from different perspectives. It is clear that, essentially, myths are modes of understanding the divine in terms of human transcendence-experience, which are closest in kind to the object it tries to grasp. And this mode of understanding cannot be communicated by everyday object-language. The relation between language and the theological venture is discussed in other sections of this work. At present, we will remain content with Macquarrie's specific remarks on myth.

We find a clear list of the attributes of myth in *God-Talk*.[6] Myths are:
1) Dramatic
2) Connotative in content rather than denotative; hence, they are evocative. They call forth imaginative responses.
3) Recognized as immediately true (i.e., are not recognized as myth of symbol).

4) Alogical (i.e., like dreams, they obey rules other than logic and still maintain coherency and significance).
5) Involved in supernatural action, good *or* bad. The elimination of this aspect of myth causes a lapse into positivism.
6) Remote in time and space. They are outside of historical time.
7) Related to community by serving as a cohesive force.

These attributes of myths are constitutive of all Biblical myths with the exception of 6) above: Biblical myths are deliberately historical.[7] This latter exception is profoundly important in respect to our view of the historical truth-claims involved in such myth, since we are obliged to distinguish between factual claims and other truths couched in language-forms which are not intended to assert objective facts. This leaves us with the double task of discerning the objective-historical which shapes the context of the myth as well as discerning the truths conveyed by the myth without reducing the myth to something it is not. This requires a healthy appreciation of the mythological forms as a purveyor of truth as well as a capacity to find those truths within that can be translated into other forms, such as objective-historical language. This double task achieves supreme importance in the Biblical myths, because their historical claims are asserted to be the ground of accepting the truths they most intently want to convey.

Macquarrie seems to recognize this quite clearly when he asserts that myths are only *in part*, albeit the most important and dominant part, an expression of self-understanding. Myths are not fully comprehended by their "anthropological" aspect and, thus, cannot be fully translated into existential self-understanding. The eschatological myths, e.g., are about time and history and cannot be ultimately reduced to a form of self-understanding, since these always transcend man's understanding.[8]

Macquarrie also distinguishes between myth and both legends and cosmologies. He defines a legend as a story that illustrates a central myth and says they should not be taken as stories in themselves.[9] It is not clear from his writings which of the stories about Jesus, for example, he would count as legends without historical import. He never offers a list of these, perhaps leaving such work to the expertise of Biblical critics.

He does admit, however, that myth includes elements of primitive science. But a myth is, basically, an undifferentiated matrix of meaning which contains many "equiprimordial" elements that can be sorted out only upon analysis. Thus, a cosmology can be seen as a primitive science fused with other elements in the undifferentiated matrix of myth.[10] It would seem that the theologian has the duty of discerning and distinguishing facts of science, even modern scientific understandings, from the other elements of myth, as well as that of relating such understanding to the truths conveyed in myth.

But Macquarrie does not pursue this sort of analysis. For him, demythologizing does not mean translating a myth into scientific language. It is quite proper to maintain myths in their symbolic form.[11] The reason for this seems to be that a mythical form is essential or necessary for conveying the *mystery* of divine activity.[12] We cannot, e.g., translate into common language, "existential statements", or scientific assertions the claim that God has acted in Jesus Christ. We *must* express this assertion in mythical terms (i.e., in symbols).[13] Indeed, Macquarrie asserts that we are not able to translate fully any myth into non-mythological language, because no language which purports to speak of God can completely rid itself of symbolic statements about God (though we can get rid of unconscious and unnecessary symbolism).[14]

Macquarrie's assertion that myth must remain to some degree an element of Christian language does not, however, mean that he rejects a degree of demythologization as a legitimate enterprise in theology. Instead, he proposes that demythologization proceed with the aim of clarifying the meaning of the gospel message[15] within the parameters of a caveat that *no* technique of demythologization can or ought to aim at a total eradication of myth. The *Kerygma*, even if it involves myth and paradox, is essential to Christianity. And, whereas an existential interpretation of it may be of basic importance in Christian thought,[16] such that there can be an existential theology, the *kerygma* and its attending myths cannot be reduced to a theology of existence.[17]

But a purely existential theology attempts to translate language about the objective-historical events of the New Testament into statements about the possibility of forgiveness and new life. It tries, i.e., to capture the *significance* of the objective-historical events, which is expressed in terms which we can understand as living, valuing, choosing, historical beings: it reduces the objective-historical to the "existential"-historical.[18]

The advantage of a wide-ranging program of demythologization is that it makes theology "intelligible", since it does not stray from the familiar territory of human experience. But, for this reason, a demythologized theology says nothing about God: it is not God-talk. And, in so far as an extensive program of demythologization tends to view God as myth, it threatens the whole enterprise of theology.[19]

In view of this damaging potential of demythologization, Macquarrie explicitly raises the issue of the limits of it:

> Is the record of events contained in the gospel narrative to be regarded as a kind of ladder, by way of which we can be brought into an understanding of religious truth? Is this understanding reached when the record ceases to be a record and is translated into a possibility of existence? The cross of Christ, for instance, may cease to be understood as an event of two thousand years ago and may become understood as a possibility confronting us now . . . But when this self-understanding

is attained, does the objective event of which the record speaks no longer matter?[20]

And he proceeds to question whether demythologization takes Christian understanding in the direction of a *gnosis*.[21]

Macquarrie wants, then, to set a limit to demythologization. We must acknowledge that the *kerygma* is the decisive act of God in Christ, an act which cannot be cast out along with myth. Acknowledging this limit to demythologization will protect against the consequences of a wholesale application of it and the consequent reduction of theology to philosophy.[22] He says,

> Hence we conclude that even if it were possible to translate all statements about the activity of God into statements about the existence of man in relation to God, it would still not be possible to get away from symbols, or from myths which are constructed out of symbols. We therefore reject the project of a demythologized Bible.[23]

Notes

1. John Macquarrie, *Thinking About God* (London, 1975), pp. 58—59.
2. John Macquarrie, *The Scope of Demythologizing: Bultmann and his Critics* (London, 1960), p. 209.
3. *Ibid.*, p. 209.
4. John Macquarrie, *Studies in Christian Existentialism* (London, 1966), p. 118.
5. Macquarrie, *Thinking About God*, pp. 36—37.
6. John Macquarrie, *God-Talk* (London, 1967), pp. 171—178.
7. *Ibid.*, pp. 158—180.
8. *Ibid.*, pp. 185—189.
9. Macquarrie, *The Scope of Demythologizing*, p. 210.
10. *Ibid.*, p. 213.
11. *Ibid.*, p. 206.
12. John Macquarrie, *An Existentialist Theology: A Comparison of Heidegger and Bultmann* (London, 1955), p. 184.
13. *Ibid.*, p. 177.
14. Macquarrie, *The Scope of Demythologizing*, p. 215.
15. Macquarrie, *God-Talk*, p. 36.
16. John Macquarrie, *Existentialism* (Middlesex, England, 1972), p. 35.
17. Macquarrie,. *The Scope of Demythologizing*, p. 152 and pp. 130—153.
    We cannot reduce the *Kerygma* to a philosophy. Even if existitentialism can give us an insight into our fallenness as well as into "authentic" existence, we are so radically alienated from such existence that we cannot of ourselves attain it. Only an act of grace from beyond ourselves can enable us to exist authentically. This grace is resident within the *kerygma* (p. 143). This point constitutes Macquarrie's critique of Fritz Buri.
18. Macquarrie, *An Existentialist Theology*, p. 175.
19. Macquarrie, *God-Talk*, p. 37.
20. Macquarrie, *The Scope of Demythologizing*, p. 20.

21. *Ibid.*, p. 21.
22. *Ibid.*, pp. 12—13.
23. John Macquarrie, *The Principles of Christian Theology*, rev. ed. (London, 1977), p. 175.

Appendix C: Macquarrie's Stand Against Speculative Thought

Macquarrie's view that understanding procedes from human existence *via* phenomenological ontology to a comprehension of emergent, hierarchically ordered realities is not seen as speculative philosophy. Existentialism is not speculative metaphysics but rather a philosophical understanding of man's own understanding of his being;[1] and this non-speculative thread runs through the whole of his comprehension of reality. By "speculative" Macquarrie means a comprehensive world-view that is projected intellectually as the fullest available explanation of reality. Speculation is an act of the intellect that is not grounded in the manifestation of Being in human existence but is an intellectual adventure *without* firm grounding.

According to Macquarrie, all forms of idealism and materialism are speculative philosophies which try to fit man into a particular comprehensive world-view; and, for this reason, they are not properly grounded in existential and phenomenological analysis. Indeed, the issue of whether the world is indeed ideal or material cannot be settled on the level of existential analysis. To say that they represent specualtive questions is to say that we cannot justifiably make such intellectual commitments.

On the grounds of such an anti-speculative stand, Macquarrie easily avoids the errors of idealism and materialism. He says that philosophies which make "spirit" their fundamental category (understood as a moral, intellectual, and personal force in the cosmos) tend to be too intellectual, speculating beyond the bounds of experience. An ungrounded abstract intellectualism does not grasp reality "as it is", nor does a "panpsychism" which is often a part of such philosophies. In general, bad arguments are at the root of these metaphysical philosophies, though plausible arguments *might* be offered on their behalf. Philosophies of spirit do have much that is good in them in that they point toward later developments in existential philosolphy! But their *tendency* is toward an ungrounded intellectualism.[2]

This tendency shows up most clearly in forms of absolute idealism. Absolute idealism, a philosophy we do not espouse today, manifests nevertheless the "speculative sin" in the fullest. It suffers from the weight of its own demand for perfection: just as its universe must be perfect, so must the philosophy which represents it. Yet many philosophies have successfully criticizes a number of weaknesses in its monistic doctrine, together with its attending emphases upon universals and optimism, as well as various other metaphysical assumptions. The fall of any one of these constitutes the fall of absolute idealism, which requires a perfect system of philosophy.[3] This way of criticizing absolute idealism (i.e., criticizing particular doctrines) may not *disprove* it, but it shows that it is rightly abandoned.[4] This form of speculation serves pure consistency rather than the question of truth, which is the far more important one. Macquarrie's statements concerning absolute idealism give us some insight into the more egregious errors of speculation.

The scope of the error of speculation for the sake of consistency may be seen in the light of some of the critical statements of it made by competing ways of thinking. Personal idealism, which remains quite close to its parent form of idealism, tried to tie a God-centered monism to our spiritual experience of that which is most closely linked to God's nature: the person. The person was abstracted out of a monism and given a pre-eminence which made it irreducible. The person could no longer be understood as a "part" of God, as it is in absolute idealism.[5] The exigencies of understanding God in terms of an impersonal monism led to a personalism which could not be re-absorbed into a purely rational monistic system. Speculation reached its critical limits and actually caused the collapse of the system it was trying to establish.

Pragmatism, realism, and analysis perform together a more wideranging critique of all forms of idealism. Pragmatism, e.g., acknowledges that we are more than rational or contemplative beings; we are also willing and acting beings. And these latter qualities are better guides to understanding than pure thought.[6] Realism and analysis make impossible the wide-sweeping assertions of idealism because of an emphasis upon analytic clarification and "external" reality.[7] Of course, these modes of doing philosophy tend to slip back into an old form of naturalism through the assumption that truth can only be found in science. Such an assumption, Macquarrie believes, makes religion only a tenuous possibility or else excludes it altogether.[8] It ends up being a speculative metaphysic in itself.[9]

More recent forms of naturalism, such as process philosophy, do not escape this criticism. Macquarrie singles out process philosophy as an example of a form of naturalism which admits such speculative errors. He views process philosophy as a non-dualistic, naturalist philosophy that has a hold on contemporary thought because it takes science, time, and becoming seriously. In so far as it does so, Macquarrie seems to be impressed by it. But he rails against its use in theology, because process philosophers view God as involved in and affected by the events of time and history in a manner which involves Him in relativity while preserving some sort of uniqueness and "insurpassibility". This presents the theologian with the problem of reconciling this latter idea of classical theism with notions of temporality and becoming. Macquarrie evidently believes this problem may prove fatal to process thought and makes it tenuous at best. His source for this judgment, however, seems to be the work of Teilhard de Chardin, whose philosophy, he claims, suffers from philosophical weakness, ambiguity, and the above-stated problem.[10] Though one can appreciate his critique of naturalism as tending toward a speculative reductionism, one must question whether his indictment of process philosophy, found only briefly mentioned in his works, might be premature, particularly as his source seems to be only that form of it found in Chardin. I do not intend to enter here into a justification of process philosophy. But I do wish to note that Macquarrie's judgment is based on flimsy grounds and that we must be prepared to consider concepts proposed by process philosophers anew and in the light of their adequacy in terms of existential analysis. We must also be prepared to consider process concepts as possibly relevant to whatever Macquarrie takes to be science; i.e., they may be relevant to what we consider to be a "fact".

Notes

1. John Macquarrie, *An Existentialist Theology: A Comparison of Heidegger and Bultmann* (London, 1955), p. 32.
2. John Macquarrie, *Twentieth-Century Religious Thought: the Frontiers of Philosophy and Theology, 1900—1960* (London, 1963).
3. Ibid., p. 43.
4. Ibid., p. 44.
5. Ibid., p. 43.
6. Ibid., p. 43.
7. Ibid., p. 44.
8. Ibid., pp. 238—239.
9. William James, *Pragmatism and Other Essays* (New York, 1968), pp. 85—86.
10. John Macquarrie, *New Directions in Theology Today: Vol. III: God and Secularity* (London, 1968), pp. 94—95.

Appendix D: Christology

The result of Macquarrie's ambiguity concerning the nature of historical facts may be even more clearly seen in his Christology. For facts seem to disappear altogether in favour of an existential-ontological interpretation of so-called "events". The historical Jesus remains a mere "horizon" for interpretation.

We can begin by analyzing the existential approach and then integrating it with the ontological assessment of the reality of Christ. We can then look at several Christological doctrines to see how the existential-ontological interpretation works itself out.

Macquarrie begins with an existential interpretation of the person of Christ. This means that we approach him in the context of an existential commitment to him, wherein we recognize him as our "ultimate concern".[1] By approaching the question "Who is Jesus?" in this way, we find in the story of his life and work something which puts us in touch with our true (authentic) selves, which Macquarrie seems to identify with being put in touch with God.[2] He explicitly excludes any "search for the historical Jesus", except in a very limited way. For he says that the historical Jesus is nearly impossible to know, except for a few things which might reasonably be accepted on the basis of historical testimony and are not shrouded in legend or myth. Macquarrie does not give an exhaustive list of acceptable historical facts, though he asserts that we must preserve at least the historical reality of Jesus.[3]

This does not mean that we can consider the Biblical claims about Jesus so discredited as to render history useless. The events as recorded are essential, even if they can be properly understood only when existentially interpreted, Macquarrie says that events such as the passion and cross are the main points of the gospel story because they keep the existential dimension of this work and being open. Certainly, we want to avoid making our Christology the function of some sort of metaphysical philosophy: "Christology becomes artificial when it becomes immersed in metaphysical distinctions about how Christ is constituted and neglects to consider what he does".[4]

The key to a correct historical approach to Jesus seems to be what Macquarrie calls "repetitive thinking".[5] Repetitive thinking is a special case of existential thinking. In it we bring an historical event to life again by thinking into it in such a way as to think it again with the agent or author.[6] This presupposes, of course, that the event is not a miracle in the true sense of the word and that the thoughts and intentions of the original historical characters can be captured in ordinary human thought. One would think that this sort of thinking could understand only in a limited way an historical event in which God himself has touched the world. But Macquarrie asserts that language, when it is expanded beyond normal usage to include the special non-literal terms employed in myth, can grasp what is essential in the Christ-event itself: not the physical being, the genes, the flesh, etc., of Christ, but his *meaning* as the center of an event that extends through space and time.[7]

This meaning can be grasped by human thought, however, precisely because it is intended for human beings. Christ is the truth in a practical sense; i.e., he is reliable and can be trusted as a guide to the way of life which leads human beings to true personhood and meaningful existence. The meaning of Christ is not so much a mysterious, complex, strange message from God but lies simply in the fact that he has brought true humanity out of concealment into the light. He shows us what we have it in us to become. There is nothing in Christ other than that which *can* be in man and which his intellect can grasp as a possibility. In Christ we are able to see that the expression of true humanity is the attainment of a condition in which the highest possibilities of our human nature will find their fullest expression.[8]

It is only because Jesus Christ is the "true man" in this sense that he is seen as the best clue to the creative reality at the heart of our universe, the truth of God. Thus, Jesus reveals the "meaning" or Word of God.[9] This word is not some kind of *gnosis*, or secret knowledge, but rather an expanded vision of what it means to be human. And this in itself is identified as new light and new insight into the Mystery of God.[10]

The import of what Macquarrie is saying here seems to be that the divinity of Christ (indeed, the divinity of God) is understood only in terms which, as symbols, refer without content to God *as an empty horizon of meaning* and *with* content only in so far as they refer to the nature of man, both in actuality and potentiality. It becomes difficult to understand in this case how Christ reveals anything of God in so far as God is distinct and other than what man is. The distinction seems to be erased; man is, *per humanitas*, already God *in potentia*; and God, *per divinitas*, is nothing but man *in toto actu*. The end point of the process of reaching our full potential remains as obscure in Macquarrie's theology as the God whose meaning it is intended of fully manifest. And God is understood only in so far as this journey is complete, and only in so far as true humanity is revealed. Macquarrie sums this point up quite well in his own words:

> But the historical symbol has also an ontological import. If history is through and through existential, that is to say, if it has to do not with mere happening but with existence in its acting, becoming, and being, then the theme of history is personal being. The historical symbol is a personal symbol, and, . . . Christ is seen as the fulfillment of selfhood, of that potentiality for a truly personal being which is the

> potentiality given with existence. But then we have already seen that personal being is the most appropriate symbol for Being itself; for personal being stands highest in that hierarchy of beings which seek to be like God, and personal being, as showing the richest diversity in unity and the highest possibilities for creativity and love, gives to our minds the fullest disclosure of the mystery of Being that we can recieve.[11]

Thus, Christ manifests Being (the ontological dimension of revelation). His humanity and divinity become identified,[12] though the *meaning* of this identification can be stated only in terms which describe *human* advancement. This is done, Macquarrie says, to avoid reducing Christ to an academic exercise and becoming embroiled in metaphysical speculation.[13]

Macquarrie, however, does ontologize his understanding of Christ and asserts that the God he manifests is something *other* than all creation, including man. The Son, the second person of the Trinity, is called "expressive Being". The energy of primordial Being is poured out through expressive Being, giving rise to particular beings that are intelligible in terms of space and time. Being mediates itself through beings, which pass temporally in and out of being. The Word, the Logos, is the agent of the Father. *He is not identified with the beings that are created* and through which he expresses himself as Being "in" beings. The Logos is part of the eternal structure of Being and is "eternally begotten".[14]

Being, then, finds "signal" expression in the person of Jesus Christ. The existential approach to an understanding of who Jesus is must include this ontological claim, which is equally primordial and necessary as the existential claim in Christology.[15] But, if it does, then we ought to be equally obliged to justify the claim that Jesus, as the creative Logos, is *other* than created beings. And this would apparently involve some sort of language which describes Being, or God, in terms other than those which apply to man or refer to a comprehensible potential of man. If Macquarrie would truly avoid metaphysics (which his own ontology of the Trinity certainly is) and describe God and the divine aspect of Christ in terms which refer only to man's potential for being, then the claim that Being is *other* than man remains an empty claim, a reference without an object. He can, of course, claim that God or Being is mysterious and defies description beyond the human-centered language he has chosen; but this claim does not in itself justify his claim of ontological difference, since the unfathomability of mystery does not rely on ontological difference. Man, e.g., is, as Gabriel Marcel has pointed out,[16] something of a mystery to himself because he always "encroaches" on the data he is studying when he seeks to understand himself and not because he suffers from some sort of ontological difference within himself. The claim of difference requires a language which describes Being in terms other than human ones, even if we cannot escape understanding Being from a finite, human perspective. But

Macquarrie would brand this precisely the sort of metaphysics he is trying to avoid.

We can see the effects of Macquarrie's "existentializing" of Christology as we look at several important Christological doctrines. The incarnation can be understood in terms of the typical Being-being relation that defines every human person. In the case of Christ, however, Being is manifested in its personal, human perfection in the being of Jesus. In this sense, he is "consubstantial with the Father";[17] and, in the "letting-be" of creation,[18] "Being reveals itself as both transcendent and immanent, and this is implied in the central Christian idea of incarnation".[19] The difference here seems to be one of degree rather than a qualitative difference. And this makes Jesus comprehensible as an incarnation of what I might become.

Of course, Macquarrie says that the incarnation is a mystery of faith. But he does not mean in saying this that Jesus refers to a qualitative distinction between God and man. He means that the truth that is manifested in Jesus' humanity is so deep that it cannot be exhausted or spoken of adequately in everyday terms. God was in Christ and, *in a sense*, Christ was God.[20] The sense in which Christ was God seems to be the participative one: being participates in Being, so that the quality of the particular being is in some way donated by the quality of Being. Thus, being reflects the greater power of Being and, in the case of man, has potential of reflecting Being with greater scope and power through some sort of progressive development. The mystery of the incarnation seems to lie in the inexpressible significances inhering in the end point of this progressive journey, which end point Jesus the man manifests. And because the journey is qualitatively similar from beginning to end by virtue of its character as a transformation of human being, not into something else, but into something perfectly human, the mystery of the incarnation is robbed of the element of otherness which Macquarrie indicates ought to be a part of it and which is clearly suggested by the non-human entities created by God. The non-human parts of creation are not necessarily less than human[21] and manifest aspects of God's Being which are qualitatively other than human characteristics of being. Indeed, the mystery of the incarnation requires for its unending unfoldment a development of symbols which refer to God, not only in His personal Being and in His personal and qualitatively continuous relationship with man (which Macquarrie has focussed on in his Christology) but in His total creative relationship with the cosmos. Macquarrie, on the contrary, seems to believe that Christ discloses the mystery of Being only in the sense of disclosing the potential of man, and this seems to compromise seriously any ordinary understanding of miracle and such aspects of God's Being as providence.[22]

One cannot speak of the incarnation without mentioning the doctrine of the virgin birth. Whatever status this controversial doctrine may end up having in Christian theology, Macquarrie has already cleared the way, following Bultmann, for an existential interpretation of it which no longer relies on any explicit acknowledgement that it corresponds to a divine-historical act. He says that it is not a biological statement of fact but is a way of indicating that God took the initiative in the incarnation. Macquarrie inserts a spiritual dynamic to explain the nature of conception: the Holy Spirit, whose function is to unite beings in being, calls Mary in her freedom to unite with God in His initiation of this event.[23] The issue whether the event occurred as a concrete historical reality is left a little less than open because of his flat denial that the virgin birth is a "biological" fact; and any further speculation on the matter seems to be blocked in favor of an existential interpretation which purports to capture the meaning of the event. But if the event is also "biological", which is an issue that is at best only side-stepped in Macquarrie's analysis, then the essential meaning includes this fact. But even if only an exercise of imagination and speculation alone can enrich our understanding until more profound thought can gain greater clarity in this issue, one ought to state the historical dimension of this truth.

Macquarrie's commitment to an existential-ontological approach affects his judgment on the historical nature of the vocation of Jesus and the transfiguration event. Influenced by Bultmann, Macquarrie seems to believe that since these stories must be mythical in the sense of excluding any concrete divine historical act, another explanation must be given. Thus, the baptism of Jesus does not occur before his ministry begins but is a reading-in of Christ's motives and actions *after* the fact of his ministry. His vocation was actually something that occurred to him as his life and ministry unfolded, something gradually called forth by the "unitive" (in this sense, "integrative") power of the Holy Spirit.[24] The transfiguration is the prime symbol of the disciples' recognition of Jesus as the suffering Christ and may be the church's account of a post-resurrection story.[25]

It is not my intention to critique the conclusions of higher Biblical criticism in this work. Such criticism is essential for understanding scripture, and I cannot in this work offer proper evidence either to confirm or deny its conclusions. But one can accept its conclusions as part of an on-going process of determining the historical as well as the existential and ontological truths without closing the matter in such a way as to leave only the existential truth as the determinative symbol. Macquarrie's way of dealing with the results of Biblical criticism seems to preclude raising the historical question again in the light of new evidence and, like Bultmann, seems to proceed on the basis of philosophical presuppositions concerning God and ultimate reality which predispose one to reject any interpretation of events which describes divine events in concrete, historical terms. Macquarrie functions for the most part on the principle that, if an event involves divine operation, then such action on the part of God is unobservable in real history and can be understood only existentially. Even the acceptable historical claims about Jesus have "real" meaning in terms of their existential interpretation. Thus, Macquarrie says that the passion and death of Christ, in its real meaning, could not have been observed by anyone at that time. What really happened is that there God acted in a way that is visible only to faith. God's reconciliation is not dependant on a complex historical happening.[26] Of course, Macquarrie believes that the cross is an historical event; but its significance lies in what it reveals about his humanity and his faith as well as in the way it opens up the existential meaning for us of his life and work.[27] Again, the historical importance of the revelation of God in Christ ("When the time had fully come, God sent forth his son"—Galatians 4:4) is not discernible in history itself but is a claim made by faith.[28]

This strong thread of existential reductionism is found alongside other elements in Macquarrie's theology which indicate a potential for a more comprehensive integration of his thought with non-existential assertions. He says, e.g., that Christ is the truth in an absolute sense: the study of who Christ is merges with the investigation into the question of truth. Since the truth about Christ is that he reveals the potential of man, then Christ is the fulfilled man made unhidden. So he becomes our goal, our end. In Christ is a givenness of our possible fulfillment, which we can see well enough to begin aiming at such being in ourselves. But since we are part of an intricate and interdependent system we call nature, and he stands at the head of the hierarchy of things, he is the head of the cosmos, the Truth of the cosmos. He therefore makes unhidden the meaning of the process of nature and should be viewed as the "deepest and truest truth".[29] He is the agent of creation as well as its prototype and is the meaning and goal of the cosmos.[30] This statement cannot help being metaphysical in precisely the sense which Macquarrie tries to avoid in so much of his theology. But it remains an undeveloped theme in his thought, perhaps because he wishes to avoid the "speculative" thought and imaginative adventures which might enrich this insight. Nonetheless, the potential for its development, even if it runs contrary to his emphasis of thought, ought to be pursued.

Notes

1. Macquarrie seems here to be borrowing Paul Tillich's language from such works as *The Courage to Be* (New Haven & London, 1952), pp. 47 & 82.
2. John Macquarrie, *Studies in Christian Existentialism* (London, 1966), p. 120.
3. John Macquarrie, *Principles of Christian Theology* (London, 1977), pp. 273—279.
4. Ibid., p. 287.

5. Macquarrie seems to be borrowing this term from Soren Kierkegaard's use of it in several works, including one entitled *Repetition*.
6. *Principles*, p. 92.
7. John Macquarrie, *The Humility of God* (London, 1978), p. 25.
8. Ibid., p. 30.
9. Ibid., p. 31.
10. John Macquarrie, *The Faith of the People of God: A Lay Theology* (London, 1972), p. 31.
11. *Principles*, p. 272.
12. Ibid., p. 296.
13. Ibid., pp. 295—296.
14. Ibid., pp. 199—200.
15. Ibid., p. 294.
16. Cf., *The Mystery of Being*.
17. *Christian Existentialism*, p. 120.
18. *Principles*, p. 299.
19. Ibid., p. 165.
20. *Humility*, p. 26.
21. E.g., angels, which Macquarrie admits might exist.
22. *Principles*, p. 271.
23. Ibid., pp. 280—282.
24. Ibid., pp. 282—284.
25. Ibid., p. 286.
26. Ibid., p. 314. Here Macquarrie seems to deny explicitly that the passion and resurrection, even if they are historical events, are in themselves effective as a power in history for salvation. Only an existential appropriation of the event through faith is efficacious for salvation.
27. Ibid., pp. 287—288.
28. Ibid., p. 270.
29. John Macquarrie, *Thinking About God* (London, 1975), pp. 21—22.
30. *Faith*, p. 54.

Bibliography

Macquarrie, John.
  An Existentialist Theology: A Comparison of Heidegger and Bultmann. London: SCM Press, Ltd., 1955.
  Christian Hope. Oxford: A.R. Mowbray & Co., Ltd., 1980.
  Christian Unity and Christian Diversity. London: SCM Press, 1975.
  Existentialism. Middlesex, England: Penguin Books, Ltd., 1972.
  God-Talk: An Examination of the Language and Logic of Theology. London: SCM Press, Ltd., 1967.
  In Search of Deity: An Essay in Dialectical Theism. London: SCM Press, Ltd., 1984.
  In Search of Humanity: A Theological and Philosophical Approach. New York, New York: The Crossroad Publishing Co., 1983.
  Martin Heidegger. London: Lutterworth Press, 1968.
  New Directions in Theology Today: Vol. III: God and Secularity. London: Lutterworth Press, 1968.
  Paths and Spirituality. London: SCM Press, Ltd., 1972.
  Principles of Christian Theology, revised edition. London: SCM Press, Ltd., 1977.
  Studies in Christian Existentialism. London: SCM Press, Ltd., 1966.
  The Concept of Peace. London: SCM Press, Ltd., 1973.
  The Faith of the People of God: A Lay Theology. London: SCM Press, Ltd., 1972.
  The Humility of God. London: SCM Press, Ltd., 1978.
  The Scope of Demythologizing: Bultmann and his Critics. London: SCM Press, Ltd., 1960.
  Thinking About God. London: SCM Press, Ltd., 1975.
  Three Issues in Ethics. London: SCM Press, Ltd., 1970.
  Twentieth-Century Religious Thought: the Frontiers of Philosophy and Theology, 1900—1960. London: SCM Press, Ltd., 1963.
  In Search of Deity: An Essay in Dialectical Theism. London: SCM Press, Ltd., 1984.

Books by authors other than Macquarrie

Ayer, A.J. *Language, Truth, and Logic*. New York: Dover Publications, 1946.
Aristotle. *Nicomachaen Ethics*. (trans. by Martin Ostwald). New York: Bobbs-Merrill Co., Inc., 1962.
  Metaphysics (trans. by Richard Hope). Ann Arbor: U. of Michigan Press, 1966.
Augustine. *Confessions of Augustine* (trans. by John K. Ryan). Garden City, N.Y.: Image Books (Doubleday & Co.), 1960.
  On Free Choice of the Will (trans. by Anna S. Benjamin and L.H. Hackstaff). Indianapolis and New York: The Bobbs-Merrill Co., Inc., 1964.
Camus, Albert. *L'Homme Révolté*. Paris: Gallimard, 1951.

Flew, Anthony and MacIntyre, eds. *New Essays in Philosophical Theology.* London: SCM Press, 1955.

Heidegger, Martin. *Being and Time* (trans. by John Macquarrie and Edward Robinson). London: Harper & Row, Publishers, 1962.

An Introduction to Metaphysics (trans. by Ralph Manheim). Garden City, N.Y.: Doubleday & Co., Inc., 1961.

Was Ist Metaphysik. Tübingen: Max Niemeyer Verlag, 1954.

Husserl, Edmund. *Ideas: General Introduction to Pure Phenomenology.* (trans. by W.R. Boyce Gibson) London: Collier Macmillan, 1975.

James, William. *Pragmatism and Other Essays.* New York: Washington Square Press, 1968.

Jaspers, karl. *The Perennial Scope of Philosophy.* London: Routledge & Kegan Paul, 1950.

Kant, Immanuel. *Religion Within the Limits of Reason Alone.* (trans. by Theodore M. Greene and Hoyt H. Hudson). New York: Harper & Row, 1960.

Kierkegaard, Soren. *Either/Or, Vol. II.* (trans. by Walter Lowrie). Garden City, N.Y.: Doubleday & Co., 1959.

Marcel, Gabriel. *Being and Having.* Glasgow: Robert Malehause & Co., University Press, 1949.

The Mystery of Being, Vol. I: Reflection and Mystery. Chicago: Henry Regnery Co., 1950.

Mascall, E.L. *He Who Is.* London: Darton, Longman, & Todd, 1950 (New Ed.).

Moore, G.E. *Principia Ethica.* Cambridge: Cambridge U. Press, 1903.

Otto, Rudolph. *The Idea of the Holy.* (trans. by John W. Harvey). London: Oxford University Press, 1971.

Pannenburg, Wolfhart. *Jesus, God and Man.* (trans. by Lewis L. Wilkins and Duane A. Priebe). London: SCM Press, Ltd., 1968.

Pears, David. *Wittgenstein.* New York: Collins, 1971.

Plato. *The Republic of Plato* (trans. by F.M. Cornford) London: Oxford U. Press, 1945.

Polanyi, Michael. *The Tacit Dimension.* Garden City, N.Y.: Doubleday & Co., 1967.

Popper, Karl. *Objective Knowledge.* Oxford: Oxford U. Press, 1972.

Rawls, John. *A Theory of Justice.* Cmabridge, Mass.: Harvard U. Press, 1971.

Ross, David (Sir). *The Foundation of Ethics.* London: Oxford U. Press, 1939.

Sartre, Jean-Paul. *Being and Nothingness.* (trans. by Hazel Barnes). New York: Simon & Schuster (Pocket Books ed.), 1978.

Tillich, Paul. *The Courage to Be.* New Haven: Yale Univ. Press, 1952.

Wisdom, John. *Philosophy and Psychoanalysis.* Oxford: Blackwell, 1953.

Wittgenstein, Ludwig. *Philosophical Investigations* (3rd ed.). (trans. by G.E.M. Anscombe) U.S.: Macmillan Co., 1969.